Tech Units and Stories

Find over 20 units that will engage your students and over 100 videos and handouts

Chris Clementi M.Ed.

Copyright © 2015 by Chris Clementi

All rights reserved. This book is intended to be used by one teacher. Resources on the sites can be shared with his/her students. Resources on the bonus sites are to be used by the teacher and his/her students only. Every precaution has been taken in the production of this book to respect copyright laws. The publisher and author take no responsibility for errors. No liability can be assumed for any possible problems that might result from the use of this book. It is the user's responsibility to pre-screen sites prior to demonstration with students.

Library of Congress Control Number: 2015914981

CreateSpace Independent Publishing Platform, North Charleston, SC

Comments

Brandi, Teacher, Colorado

"I am always amazed at how willing you are to help others. The amount of information you share with our staff is above and beyond. Thanks for helping!"

Jessica, Student, Colorado

"Thank you for helping me the other day with our Switch Zoo project. It meant a lot. You're the best teacher I have ever had. You make me smile every day with your videos and your smile, even when I feel tired or sad. Happy Valentines Day!"

John, Teacher, Arkansas

"Your book has really helped out in my classroom! I also teach middle school computers and it's been a huge help!"

Vanessa, Student, Colorado

"When I walk into your room, I am inspired. When I wake in the morning, I think I want to be like you! You are my role-model and my superior. You are my hero."

Jennifer, Teacher, Colorado

"I am talking to my husband about the class and can't stop raving. You have a true fan in me and you should think about spreading the word even more to other schools/teachers!" (Regarding my book class)

Comments

Susan, Technology Coordinator New York

"I was looking at your Google resources and WOW!!! You are amazing."

Shayne, Art and Computer Literacy, Toronto

"I wanted to thank you for sharing your Google information with the Edtech group. I'm also a fan of your Kidsnetsoft site. I teach high-school art and computer literacy in Toronto and used your information on website evaluation and more. I appreciate all your contributions!"

William, Student, Colorado

"You always make class fun, interesting and most of all exciting."

Kendall, Student, Colorado

"You are the best computer teacher ever!"

Annette, High School Teacher, Colorado

"You are always willing to go the extra mile to make sure people know what they are doing."

Chelley, Drama Teacher, Colorado

"Chris is a dynamic, interesting teacher with extensive background knowledge."

Sarah, Student, Colorado

"Thank you for everything you've done to make computer class the ultimate experience."

Comments

Phil, Librarian and Lesley Instructor, Colorado

"Does your school realize how lucky they are to have you?"

Joy, Principal, Colorado

"Her knowledge of instructional strategies in the curricular areas of technology and information literacy makes her an exceptional teacher."

Sharolyn, Teacher

"Thanks! I received your CD last week and have already started using some ideas! Thanks for making something organized and easy to use."

Alissa, Student, Colorado

"Thank you for teaching me technology. It is a fun class and you make it more fun. You are a great teacher. Keep up the great work."

Isabel, Student, Colorado

"Thank you so much for everything you do for our school. You have a really fun class and I enjoy coming to it everyday. I never get bored. Maybe I get bored when we are typing, but you always put a smile on my face. I've always enjoyed working on computers, but you inspire me in ways I never imagined. Thanks again for everything."

Comments

Priscilla, Student, Colorado

"Thanks so much for helping me understand all about Photoshop. Without your videos and your help, I would be very confused. You're the best teacher ever. I love computer class so much. I wish this quarter would never end."

Matt, Student, Colorado

"You are the best teacher in Mountain Ridge. Thank you for making technology the best exploratory I've had. You are really nice and funny. Technology is my favorite class."

Chase, Student, Colorado

"Thank you for teaching me this year, you've been an amazing teacher."

Kayla, Student, Colorado

"Thank you for being the best technology teacher ever! I hope I am in your class next year!"

Collin, Student, Colorado

"Thank you for being such a great teacher. I really appreciate having your great class."

Alex, Student, Colorado

"You are the best computer teacher ever."

Mikayla, Student, Colorado

"You are amazing! I hope I get you next year."

Quotes

If we teach today as we taught yesterday, we rob our children of tomorrow. ~John Dewey

"There can be infinite uses of the computer and of new age technology, but if teachers themselves are not able to bring it into the classroom and make it work, then it fails." ~Nancy Kassebaum

"Teaching in the Internet age means we must teach tomorrow's skills today." ~Jennifer Fleming

"Teachers need to integrate technology seamlessly into the curriculum instead of viewing it as an add-on, an afterthought, or an event." ~Heidi-Hayes Jacobs

"We need technology in every classroom and in every student and teacher's hand, because it is the pen and paper of our time, and it is the lens through which we experience much of our world." ~David Warlick

"The real problem is not whether machines think but whether men do." ~B. F. Skinner

"We need to prepare students for their future, not our past." ~Ian Jukes

"It is important to remember that educational software, like textbooks, is only one tool in the learning process. Neither can be a substitute for well-trained teachers, leadership, and parental involvement." ~Keith Krueger

Table of Contents

Trends..1

Carp Design..2-14

Activity 1: Being Organized..............................15

Activity 2: Being Savvy Online..........................16

Activity 3: Google Searches...............................17

Activity 4: Who You Talking To?......................18

Activity 5: The Find Function...........................19

Activity 6: Reading Levels............................20-22

Activity 7: Endangered Animals..................23-25

Activity 8: Switch Zoo.................................26-27

Activity 9: PowerPoint Design....................28-30

Activity 10: Did You Know?........................31-34

Activity 11: Alphabet Literacy.....................35-37

Activity 12: Visual Literacy.........................38-43

Activity 13: Get Wise Online......................44-47

Activity 14: Pixlr Workshop........................48-51

Table of Contents

Activity 15: Fable Unit.................................52-54

Activity 16: Digital Footprint......................55-60

Activity 17: Chrome Extensions..................61-62

Activity 18: Google Drawings.....................63-67

Activity 19: Google Surveys........................68-69

Activity 20: Presentation Jeopardy..............70-71

Activity 21: Google Sites.............................72-76

Activity 22: Google Classroom....................77-80

Activity 23: Satire.......................................81-83

Activity 24: Video Resumes........................84-86

Extra Sites: Fun Links.................................87-90

Bonus Sites: Comes with purchase..............91-94

New Units: Adding New Material.................95-98

Google Apps & More: Google Resources.....99-100

Weekly Tech Tips: Tech Tips......................101-105

Notes: Add your own ideas........................106-110

How to Use This Book

I have been building tech integration curriculum since 2003. It is one of my greatest passions. When I attend a workshop that is valuable, I often end up creating an online unit. I have over 40 websites that are packed with videos, handouts, resources, examples, and more. I have over 200 Youtube videos for the education community. The Internet is truly an overwhelming place. This book is designed to help you appreciate how the units evolved and simplify rather than complicate your already busy life as an educator. Most of the activities will share a personal story based on experience with hundreds of students. When you visit my site customized for this book, you will have access to many of those units. With technology constantly changing, energy will be spent on keeping the site current. Visit my site to access all the fabulous units behind the stories. If you choose to use my resources without purchasing the book, I graciously ask for a small donation on the Purchase page. There is a link on the Home page encouraging you to submit recommended changes to the site. If you buy this book, e-mail me at **kidsnetsoft@gmail.com** to get an invitation to the Bonus Units and resources. In the subject line, type Tech Units and Stories 1617164960

To access the site, go to https://sites.google.com/site/techunitsandstories/

Acknowledgements

This book was written by me, with the help of students, family, friends, colleagues and members of online communities who create applications that make integrating technology fun, easy and exciting. My partner, Paul and daughter, Marianne have been very supportive throughout this process. I could not have done this without my students. They give me ideas that I couldn't get from a book or workshop. They help me grow as an educator and I truly appreciate them. My colleague and friend, Cris Hardin has graciously provided editing and valuable feedback on this book. I am genuinely thankful for the Open Source Community, Google and other creative sites that have made this book possible. Some of those wonderful resources include Animoto, Audacity, and Pixlr. I am grateful for Microsoft's software, which has resulted in some of the greatest projects in my classroom. I ultimately want to thank Google for their amazing contributions to the education community. Their tools have allowed my students to create, collaborate, communicate and use critical thinking skills with Google Apps. Google for Education continues to allow me to present at their summits, which has contributed to my continual growth in the field of technology integration in education.

About

I have been teaching computer design to middle school students since 2003. During that time, I have had four of my lessons published in the EdTech Magazine: Internet Hoaxes, Multimedia Projects, Global Warming and Online Culture. I acquired a Masters in Technology in Education from Lesley University. Since 2004, I have been a frequent presenter at various technology conferences in Colorado. In addition to annual presentations, I have trained staff members in numerous workshops. During the summer of 2009, I became Google Teacher Certified in Boulder. I regularly present at the Google for Education Summits in Colorado to stay current with Google tools. You can find my book "Great Ways to Integrate Technology in the Classroom" on Amazon or Infinity Publishing. I have contributed over 40 Google websites and over 200 videos have been uploaded to Youtube for the education community. I believe that to be an effective educator, you have to continually embrace new ideas by keeping as current as possible with new tools to engage students with meaningful and relevant projects.

Trends

As a teacher, I reflect on the benefits students will get from my curriculum. I place a lot of emphasis on literacy, digital skills, and fun. I do think it is imperative that students enjoy the learning process. Personally, if I am not engaged in a subject, I shut down and don't learn. Some students have actually claimed that the only important classes are math, science, history and language arts. Though I think those classes are very important, I do believe that the elective classes are equally important in the development of the whole child. This belief was confirmed after I came across an interesting article, "Diverse Conversations: Preparing Students for the Labor Force" by Matthew Lynch, Ed.D. Their findings revealed that employers want new hires that can do a little bit of everything. "In the past several years, we have seen a shift from employers demanding a focused skill set to a much broader one. For example, five years ago, reporter job postings may have sought someone who could write, conduct interviews and generate story ideas. Now, they are calling for someone who can do all those things, plus shoot video, edit, write for the web and market stories via social media." This brought a serious smile to my face because those skills are heavily emphasized in my classroom.

CARP Design

I learned about CARP Design early in my teaching career and I consistently use it with my students throughout my lessons so that they create projects that are aesthetically pleasing. CARP stands for Contrast, Alignment, Repetition and Proximity. Too often teachers will give students projects without discussing design tips. Consequently, the project might have good content, but the presentation is unappealing and often unreadable. When something is unappealing, it doesn't have the same awe factor from the audience as one that incorporates design strategies. I remember telling a teacher that her students' projects were attractive. She replied, " I don't care what they look like. I care about the content." I was dumbfounded. I truly believe both are very important. I teach both! "By creating content that is aesthetic, concise, refreshed and entertaining, your digital signage will be a hit. Spend a little extra time learning design basics, so your slides will capture the attention of your audience." Digital SignageToday

The next few pages will give more information and examples of each of the design techniques. Many of the rubrics found for the various units will incorporate design. For more depth, check out The Non-Designer's Design Book by Robin Williams.

Design Quotes

"First impressions are 94% design related." ~Kinesis

"Design is intelligence made visible." ~Alina Wheeler

"Design is the conscious effort to impose a meaningful order." ~Victor Papanek

"Good design is good business. ~Thomas J. Watson

"There is only one type of designer – the type that cares about type." ~Rohan Nanavati

"Please don't use Comic Sans-We are a Fortune 500 Company, not a lemonade stand."

"Design is thinking made visual" ~Saul Bass

"Design is a plan for arranging elements in such a way as best to accomplish a particular purpose." ~Charles Eames

"Creativity is allowing yourself to make mistakes. Design is knowing which ones to keep." ~Scott Adams

"Typography is the use of type to advocate, communicate, celebrate, edu- cate, elaborate, illuminate, and disseminate. Along the way, the words and pages become art." ~James Felici

"Bad design shouts at you. Good design is the silent seller." ~Shane Meendering

Contrast

"Contrast occurs when two elements are different. The greater the difference is the greater the contrast. The key to working with contrast is to make sure the differences are obvious." *Digest Web Design*

I always tell my students that black text on a white background is the most readable combination. It also happens to have the greatest contrast. They will often argue such a combination is boring. There are so many other ways they can add to their product to make it interesting and appealing to the reader. I emphasize they should not sacrifice readability for "interesting." When creating posters, newsletters, articles, resumes, etc., it is important to have a stronger and bolder typeface in the headlines and subheads. "A reader should always be able to glance at a document and instantly understand what is going on." During the poster unit, I emphasize they should have their title for each endangered animal pop out from the information about the animal. The following pages have an example of a poorly designed poster and a well designed poster.

*See the contrast examples by visiting the site. Click on **CARP: Design Tips** under assignments.

Contrast Example #1

This example lacks contrast. Notice the title doesn't stand out and the titles for each animal are the same font as the content.

Endangered Animals

Killer Whales: Killer whales are the largest member of the dolphin family. They can live 30 to 50 years in the wild. They eat fish, birds, squid and marine animals. They are endangered because of pollution and chemicals. The pollution leads to diseases and reproduction problems.

I love my babies

Polar Bears: Polar bears are one of the largest predators in the world. Their diet primarily consists of ringed and bearded seals. Their fur is thicker than any other bear. They are endangered because loss of sea ice which affects their hunting. They are also threatened because of illegal poaching.

What about bugs!

Tigers: Tigers are the largest of the cat family. They are strong swimmers. Their lifespan is 10-15 years. They are endangered primarily because of illegal poaching for their pelts and body parts. They are also threatened by humans encroaching on their habitat, leading to competition for resources.

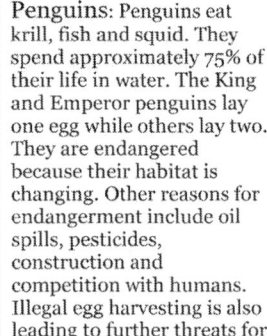

Penguins: Penguins eat krill, fish and squid. They spend approximately 75% of their life in water. The King and Emperor penguins lay one egg while others lay two. They are endangered because their habitat is changing. Other reasons for endangerment include oil spills, pesticides, construction and competition with humans. Illegal egg harvesting is also leading to further threats for the penguins.

Giant Pandas: Giant pandas are solitary animals. They don't hibernate. They spend most of their day eating. They are endangered because of habitat loss from humans competing with them for resources. They are also illegally poached.

Images from Geek Philosopher

Contrast Example #2

This example has much greater contrast than example #1. Notice the title for each animal is different than the content.

Endangered Animals

Killer Whales: Killer whales are the largest member of the dolphin family. They can live 30 to 50 years in the wild. They eat fish, birds, squid and marine animals. They are endangered because of pollution and chemicals. The pollution leads to diseases and reproduction problems.

I love my babies!

Polar Bears: Polar bears are one of the largest predators in the world. Their diet primarily consists of ringed and bearded seals. Their fur is thicker than any other bear. They are endangered because loss of sea ice which affects their hunting. They are also threatened because of illegal poaching.

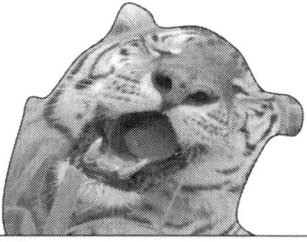

What about bugs!

Tigers: Tigers are the largest of the cat family. They are strong swimmers. Their lifespan is 10-15 years. They are endangered primarily because of illegal poaching for their pelts and body parts. They are also threatened by humans encroaching on their habitat, leading to competition for resources.

Penguins: Penguins eat krill, fish and squid. They spend approximately 75% of their life in water. The King and Emperor penguins lay one egg while others lay two. They are endangered because their habitat is changing. Other reasons for endangerment include oil spills, pesticides, construction and competition with humans. Illegal egg harvesting is also leading to further threats for the penguins.

Giant Pandas: Giant pandas are solitary animals. They don't hibernate. They spend most of their day eating. They are endangered because of habitat loss from humans competing with them for resources. They are also illegally poached.

Images from Geek Philosopher

Alignment

"Positioning elements to left, right or center will define the look of your design. Every element on the page should have a visual connection with other elements in order to have a clean, fresh and yet sophisticated layout." *Digest Web Design*

When creating a project, items should be placed with a purpose. Often, students will place items on a page because there is space. Robin Williams, designer and award winning author, recommends you either choose right or left but not center because it is old style and dull. She argues that right or left alignment gives a more sophisticated look. After reading *The Non Designers Design Book*, I tend to align my titles on the left. "You might consider it for a headline, but in general, aligning your text to the left will make your readers much more comfortable, unless they read from right to left." *webdesignerdepot.com* In addition to aligning left, I will often align along the bottom and distribute 3 or more images of equal distance apart to give the product a cleaner look.

*See the alignment examples by visiting the site. Click on **CARP: Design Tips** under assignments.

Alignment Example

This example might be considered a "weaker" design in comparison with text aligned either to the left or right. Centered text is fine for headlines and short lines of text.

About My Site:

Welcome to Ms. Clementi's Classroom. This site will showcase student assignments and sample work. Click on the different grade levels to see what they are doing. NETS standards will be posted to give you an idea how each lesson meets various performance standards that have been established by ISTE, the International Society for Technology in Education. Ms. Clementi is very dedicated to providing her students with meaningful and rich curriculum. It is imperative that students develop and appreciation for technology to enrich their academic and non academic endeavors. As you explore this site, you will see the great opportunities that her students have to learn creative ways of using technology for various purposes. If a student is really motivated, they could make a computer class portfolio.

Alignment Example

This example would be considered a "stronger" design in comparison with center alignment. It is much easier to read text aligned left then if it is centered.

About My Site:

Welcome to Ms. Clementi's Classroom. This site will showcase student assignments and sample work. Click on the different grade levels to see what they are doing. NETS standards will be posted to give you an idea how each lesson meets various performance standards that have been established by ISTE, the International Society for Technology in Education. Ms. Clementi is very dedicated to providing her students with meaningful and rich curriculum. It is imperative that students develop and appreciation for technology to enrich their academic and non academic endeavors. As you explore this site, you will see the great opportunities that her students have to learn creative ways of using technology for various purposes. If a student is really motivated, they could make a computer class portfolio.

Repetition

"Repeating visual elements such as font type, background colors, shapes, and texture helps to develop a good organization and a strong unity." *Digest Web Design.*

Repetition represents the consistency element in design. When products have a consistent theme, there is an organized look and feel to the design. I tell my students that when they have a consistent background, navigation scheme, font scheme, etc. viewers of their product will tend to focus on the content and not the sporadic changes in design. When students are creating a product, they are required to choose a consistent title font, with a heavier weight than the content. When creating products, they must keep consistent with fonts across all pages or elements of that product. For example, if they choose Georgia size 14 for their content, they must have that font choice for elements that are of equal importance. I even go as far as recommending the same transition for each slide on their PowerPoints. Students like to have inconsistencies in their design because they think it is "cool."

*See the repetition examples by visiting the site. Click on **CARP: Design Tips** under assignments.

Repetition Example

This example lacks repetition. Notice the fonts are inconsistent for the content. The images are also different sizes. The fonts for the content are also some of the most difficult to read.

WORLD CULTURES

Afghanistan: To avoid insulting people from Afghanistan, eat with your right hand, dress conservatively and remove your shoes if visiting their home. Men and women should avoid prolonged eye contact. If a man speaks directly to a woman, he is dishonoring her. Men and women should never shake hands.

ALGERIA: LIKE AFGHANISTAN, MEN SHOULD AVOID PROLONGED EYE CONTACT WITH WOMEN. THEY SHOULDN'T ASK PERSONAL QUESTIONS. IF INVITED TO THEIR HOMES, YOU SHOULD BRING FRUIT, FLOWERS OR PASTRIES. DON'T BRING VIOLETS BECAUSE THEY ARE SYMBOLIC OF SADNESS. ROSES AND TULIPS ARE CONSIDERED GOOD GIFTS. CHILDREN LIKE TO RECEIVE SWEETS. MAKE SURE YOU EAT WITH YOUR RIGHT HAND. WOMEN ESPECIALLY SHOULD DRESS CONSERVATIVELY.

AUSTRALIA: AUSTRALIANS TEND TO BE INFORMAL SO GREETINGS ARE USUALLY CASUAL. THEY PREFER CALLING PEOPLE BY THEIR FIRST NAMES. IF YOU ARE INVITED TO DINNER, YOU SHOULD BRING A BOX OF CHOCOLATES OR FLOWERS. IF INVITED TO A BBQ, YOU SHOULDN'T BE MORE THAN 15 MINUTES LATE. THEY LIKE PEOPLE WHO ARE SINCERE AND GENUINE.

Repetition Example

This example has repetition. Notice the fonts are consistent for the content. The titles are consistently the same for each culture and the images are the same size. The content is also easy to read.

World Cultures

Afghanistan: To avoid insulting people from Afghanistan, eat with your right hand, dress conservatively and remove your shoes if visiting their home. Men and women should avoid prolonged eye contact. If a man speaks directly to a woman, he is dishonoring her. Men and women should never shake hands.

Algeria: Like Afghanistan, men should avoid prolonged eye contact with women. They shouldn't ask personal questions. If invited to their homes, you should bring fruit, flowers or pastries. Don't bring violets because they are symbolic of sadness. Roses and tulips are considered good gifts. Children like to receive sweets. Make sure you eat with your right hand. Women especially should dress conservatively.

Australia: Australians tend to be informal so greetings are usually casual. They prefer calling people by their first names. If you are invited to dinner, you should bring a box of chocolates or flowers. If invited to a BBQ, you shouldn't be more than 15 minutes late. They like people who are sincere and genuine.

Proximity

"Items relating to each other should be grouped close together. This will reduce clutter. That's why we create a navigation bar rather than putting links all over the pages." *Digest Web Design.*

This design rule is often violated during classroom projects. Students will often not group related items together, causing confusion. For example, when creating the endangered poster, students might have a label for a bear touching a fox. They won't put distance between unrelated items, contributing to a misleading product. There needs to be some distance between unrelated items, often referred to as "white" space. When creating a product, there needs to be some "white" space to guide the user's eyes without overwhelming them. It becomes a fine balance where you don't want too much "white" space and you don't want clutter. By incorporating the proximity principle, the product will be more organized. If there is organization, it is more likely going to be read. Though we are discussing the proximity rule, the bad example on the next page will illustrate poor alignment and repetition as well.

*See the proximity examples by visiting the site. Click on **CARP: Design Tips** under assignments.

Proximity Example

Example # 2 has much greater proximity. Notice that the labels are sporadically placed on the slide in example 1, yet in example 2, they are consistently placed under the proper image.

Activity One

Being Organized: As a middle school teacher, one might assume students come to class with a wealth of knowledge regarding anything having to do with computers. It would almost seem a waste of time to cover organization, such a seemingly basic skill. Unfortunately, organization is not one of the skills they come equipped with. Consequently, it is one of the first activities I cover. It is one of those lessons that is emphasized consistently throughout my class. Students are expected to create a folder for activities that will be taught in class. They then create several folders for programs that might be used for units. I have them learn the basics of locating and opening programs, finding and saving images and sound. Once they open the program, they are asked to save it in the logical folder and name it according to the directions. I have had students ask, "How do I get the image of a dolphin into the images folder? I accidently put it in the sound folder." They will often save without naming or acknowledging where they are on the computer. This is a foundation that needs to be established and maintained to make life easier. Such poor organization keeps them from being efficient.

Activity Two

Being Savvy Online: It is so easy to fool people. I got the idea for this unit when I was living in Brooklyn, NY. I was working for a nonprofit in Manhattan helping teachers integrate technology in the classroom. After 9-11, an image was being circulated via e-mail with a tourist on top of the World Trade Center moments before it was tragically hit by terrorists. The image was disturbing and the e-mail circulation was unconscionable. I was a bit on the clueless side about hoaxes, but this e-mail triggered a lot of questions. I got to researching and discovered Snopes, Urban Legends, Museum of Hoaxes, Hoax Slayer and other sites that help determine if information is credible or not. Since then, I have been finding e-mail hoaxes, images and videos to share with students. Students are given the information and then must determine if the information is legitimate or not. They must use efficient key word searches and then locate credible sources to determine if the information is real or not.

> Raising student awareness to this topic is definitely a life long learning opportunity that can protect them from scams, potential harm and financial loss.

Activity Three

Google Searches: Helping students be safe online can be daunting. Even when they specify they want their images or content to be filtered, they can still get inappropriate images. This activity will give some basic tips about being safer with Google image searches. Several years ago, one of my students was looking up one of her favorite movies for a project. I didn't think to put restrictions on their key word searches. I couldn't imagine a 7th grade student would be looking up images of an rated R horror film. She clicked on the small image to get the larger quality image and saw a very inappropriate image that had nothing to do with the film. The principal and I decided to put restrictions on the type of film they look up online. They complete a plan that requires keywords for their images. I always tell my students that if inappropriate images continue to appear in a search to change their keyword search or come up with another topic to avoid inappropriate images.

> "More children and teens are being exposed to online pornography, mostly by accidentally viewing sexually explicit websites while surfing the Internet, researchers say." USA Today

Activity Four

Who You Talking To?: I made this activity a part of my online safety unit. I got the idea to do this lesson after watching the Dr. Phil show. The episode was about Catfishing. An older woman started a relationship with a man she met online. Not too long into their online relationship, the man started to ask for money. She sent money without question. She had been scammed out of thousands of dollars. I kept wondering how she could possibly be so foolish. How does someone go about sending so much money without even physically meeting someone? I was dumb founded. Out of curiosity, I took a photo of the man on the television and used a method one can use on a Google image search. After using this technique, this man's image popped up on several scam sites. The actual person was an innocent man whose identity had been stolen and used on various sites to scam gullible and naïve victims. Though this method won't work with all images, it can be helpful.

Catfish defined: "A catfish is someone who pretends to be someone they're not using Facebook or other social media to create false identities, particularly to pursue deceptive online romances." *urban dictionary*

Activity Five

The Find Function: Being efficient with saving time can reduce stress in our busy lives. When trying to locate specific information online, I will ask my students what strategies they use to find their information. Many will say they read the entire article, while others say they skim the site. Very few mention the find function. Though it is great to encourage reading, there are times when you just want answers as quickly as possible. This lesson is twofold. I take them to a fake website and have them locate information as quickly as possible. Before using my site, I would have them research a site whose URL happens to be www.idiotica.com. After having students locate information about Mars and Beluga Whales using the Find Function and using logical key words, I would call them up and tell them how disappointed I was with them. They were confused. They would ask, "Is it because we plagiarized?" "Is it because we did not cite the information?" I said no, you didn't' pay attention to where you were online. When I showed them the web address they temporarily got mad at me. It was fun! I said we will not always be so lucky to have web addresses that give away their lack of credibility.

Activity Six

Reading Levels: I got the idea to do this lesson after listening to a Social Studies teacher explain how excited her reluctant writers were when they realized they could continually check to see the improvements in reading levels after making modifications to their stories. I found a story written at a basic level for them to edit. According to Microsoft Word, the Flesh-Kincaid level wasn't even at the first grade level. I gave examples of how students can take a basic word and use Microsoft Word's built in thesaurus to swap it with a larger, more descriptive word. They were encouraged to add more adjectives and to make their sentences more complicated. I then modeled how to check the reading level after making a few changes. I had to set a few rules so they wouldn't write an unintelligible story. Before I had any rules, a student went online and found a complicated article. He incorporated it into his story by writing, "To make my day worse, I had to read the following story." He then pasted the article from the Internet into his story. This brought his Flesh-Kincaid level to 12th grade within 5 minutes. Consequently, one of the rules is they can't copy and paste from the Internet.

Activity Six: Google

Alternative Assignment: I made an assignment encouraging students to collaborate using Google Docs. I had my 7th graders invite two groups of 6th graders to work on improving the reading levels of a story. You can find a link to the online unit after clicking on Activity Six of the book website. You can even have your students invite co-editors from other schools. This unit has user friendly how-to videos to guide your students throughout the writing process. The bottom image has the website façade of the Google Docs unit.

Collaborating with Google

| Home | Agenda | Videos |

Welcome to a fun unit that will require one group of students to invite students from other classes to work on a story together. The purpose of the activity is to have each group of students improve the reading level of the story. The story they are given is written at a very basic reading level. Students will be encouraged to add more words to each sentence, change one syllable words to words that are more complicated and interesting...

Writing Example

Parts of the Original Story: I had a bad day when I woke up today. I fell out of bed and hit my head on the nightstand. I had a bad time finding my clothes. I couldn't find my pants, shirt and shoes. I had to wear dirty clothes. Other bad things continued to happen as I got ready for school. *Flesch Kincaid Grade level*: 2

Example of Modifications: I had an incredibly challenging day after I woke up this dark, depressing and gloomy morning. After my alarm went off, I fell off of my durable and inflexible mattress and smashed my head on the sharp corner of my nightstand. When I was ready to get dressed, I had a difficult time locating my clean and stylish clothes. I inspected every inch of my room, yet was still unable to find my favorite denim skirt with embroidered flowers which I could have sworn I placed on my dresser the night before. In addition to not being able to locate my skirt, I was also unable to find my apple green colored shirt and shoes that would have truly complemented my outfit. I had to wear filthy, soiled, unwashed clothes. Some other atrocious things continued to happen this morning as I got myself ready for school. *Flesch Kincaid Grade level*: 9.7

Activity Seven

Endangered Animals: I have been doing this unit since 2004. Students learned how to make attractive posters that would adhere to design techniques using Microsoft Word. They learned about various tools in Microsoft Word and how to take their notes and turn them into complete sentences. It is a fabulous unit. After attending a Google Summit in Colorado, I realized how powerful Google Drawings could be in education. I turned this same unit into a Google Drawing activity. Though each program has its pros and cons, one distinct advantage to Google Drawings is the ease with which a drawing can be added to a web page. As students make modifications in Drawings, all they have to do is refresh the web page to see the changes. Students would provide constructive feedback to their peers at the end of the unit and students would use that feedback to make the necessary modifications to improve their project. They enjoyed giving and receiving feedback. Several students went on and gave feedback to as many students as time would allow. Another great feature with the Google Drawing unit is students could add audio and video to their posters, making it more interactive and dynamic. Students recorded their voices in Audacity and then made links to the audio for viewers.

Poster Example: Word

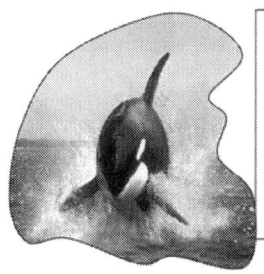

Killer Whales: Killer whales are the largest member of the dolphin family. They can live 30 to 50 years in the wild. They eat fish, birds, squid and marine animals. They are endangered because of pollution and chemicals. The pollution leads to diseases and reproduction problems.

Polar Bears: Polar bears are one of the largest predators in the world. Their diet primarily consists of ringed and bearded seals. Their fur is thicker than any other bear. They are endangered because loss of sea ice which affects their hunting. They are also threatened because of illegal poaching.

Tigers: Tigers are the largest of the cat family. They are strong swimmers. Their lifespan is 10-15 years. They are endangered primarily because of illegal poaching for their pelts and body parts. They are also threatened by humans encroaching on their habitat, leading to competition for resources.

Giant Pandas: Giant pandas are solitary animals. They don't hibernate. They spend most of their day eating. They are endangered because of habitat loss from humans competing with them for resources. They are also illegally poached.

Penguins: Penguins eat krill, fish and squid. They spend approximately 75% of their life in water. The King and Emperor penguins lay one egg while others lay two. They are endangered because their habitat is changing. Other reasons for endangerment include oil spills, pesticides, construction and competition with humans. Illegal egg harvesting is also leading to further threats for the penguins.

Microsoft Word allows students to use a variety of tools that aren't available in Google Drawings. For instance, students can draw irregular and unique shapes and add images to those shapes. The Google Drawing example has links to sites, audio, and video.

Online Poster Unit

Endangered Poster Drawings

| Home | Archive | Example | Products | Rubric | Videos |

endangered animals

Endangered Animals

Polar Bears: Polar bears are one of the largest predators in the world. Their diet primarily consists of ringed and bearded seals. Their fur is thicker than any other bear. They are endangered because of the loss of sea ice which affects their hunting. They are also threatened because of illegal poaching.

Penguins: Penguins eat krill, fish and squid. They spend approximately 75% of their life in water. The King and Emperor penguins lay one egg while others lay two. They are endangered because their habitat is changing. Other reasons for endangerment include oil spills, pesticides, construction and competition with humans. Illegal egg harvesting is also leading to further threats for the penguins.

Please help save us!

Tigers: Tigers are the largest of the cat family. They are strong swimmers. Their lifespan is 10-15 years. They are endangered primarily because of illegal poaching for their pelts and body parts. They are also threatened by humans encroaching on their habitat, leading to competition for resources.

Killer Whales: Killer whales are the largest member of the dolphin family. They can live 30 to 50 years in the wild. They eat fish, birds, squid and marine animals. They are endangered because of pollution and chemicals. The pollution leads to diseases and reproduction problems.

Activity Eight

Switch Zoo: I remember seeing young children playing on a website that allowed the user to make interesting animals. It seemed to really engage the user. I thought it would be enjoyable to have students create a creature on the site and then write a creative story about the fantasy animal. I don't know how much creative writing occurs in school, but I think it is one of those areas that needs to be encouraged in education. I ended up turning this unit into an extensive activity that requires students to create an animal and write a 200 word story that incorporates fact with fiction. Though the site might seem more relevant to elementary aged students, my 6th and 7th grade students thoroughly enjoy this unit. They use Audacity, a sound editing program, to record their story word for word and remove any imperfections. Once they record their stories, they upload them to a Voki. They use the embed code of the Voki to add to their one page website that I invite them to be editors. As editors of the website, students are able to provide constructive feedback to their peers. The purpose of the feedback is to help each other "perfect" their product. If teachers don't want to bother with the website idea or Voki, they can easily have them create a creature and then write a creative writing piece.

Online Switchzoo Unit

Online Switchzoo Unit

| Home | Archive | Example | Rubric | Student | Videos |

This unique and very interesting animal is known as the Arctic Gemswolf. It has the head of an Arctic Wolf, the body of a bison, the legs of a Gemsbok and the tail of a Collared Lizard. It can be found in the mountainous regions of Canada and the northern United States. It is a carnivore, which means it eats meat. They are known to eat caribou, oxen, birds, seals and lemmings. Its predators include grizzly bears, coyotes, gray wolves and humans. They can run as fast as 37 miles per hour. The male can weigh as much as 900 pounds while the female weighs roughly 600 pounds...

Switch Zoo allows students to create interesting animal combinations. Students are invited to a classroom website to add their one page site for others to enjoy. If creating a Google site isn't an option, you can do an alternative assignment, tapping into creative writing.

Activity Nine

PowerPoint Design: PowerPoint is used consistently in education and business. It has become redundant for many. In some circles, you could be ridiculed for using it instead of some of the free alternative applications. I would have to agree that there are some great tools that could be used in place of PowerPoint. However, I think it is important to expose students to a variety of applications so they can make a judgment call which applications are best for the creation of a final product. To me, the biggest problem with PowerPoint is that people don't incorporate design tips that could make the presentation more powerful and useful. This lesson will allow students to learn about various tools in PowerPoint that tap into their creativity. They learn shortcuts that can be very beneficial for productivity. The basics of design are emphasized continuously throughout the unit. They are discouraged from using animations unless they know what they are doing. We all know students can get a bit out of hand with animations.

"More than 120 million people are using PowerPoint to create business and educational presentations worldwide." *Doug Lowe*

Online PowerPoint Unit

Online PowerPoint Unit

| Home | Book | Design | Example | Resource | Videos |

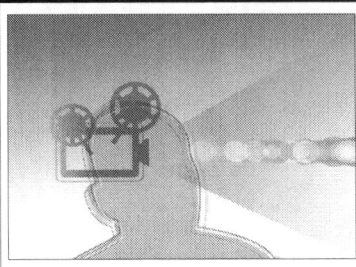

Welcome to Kidsnetsoft's PowerPoint basics workshop. This site will allow students to create aesthetically pleasing PowerPoint presentations about themselves. They will learn helpful tips on how to efficiently use PowerPoint while they learn design techniques that will maintain the interest of their audience. Before starting this production, students should create a folder and name it something like PowerPoint. It should be in a logical and safe location on their computer. Once they create the folder, they should download all the documents...

Possible Topics

Movies	Artists	Musicians	Subjects
TV Shows	Museums	Instruments	Actors
Places	Parks	Restaurants	Actresses
Hobbies	Stores	Songs	Books
Classes	Colors	Games	People
Sports	Superheroes	Flowers	Cars
Athletes	Youtubers	Animals	Characters

Slide Examples

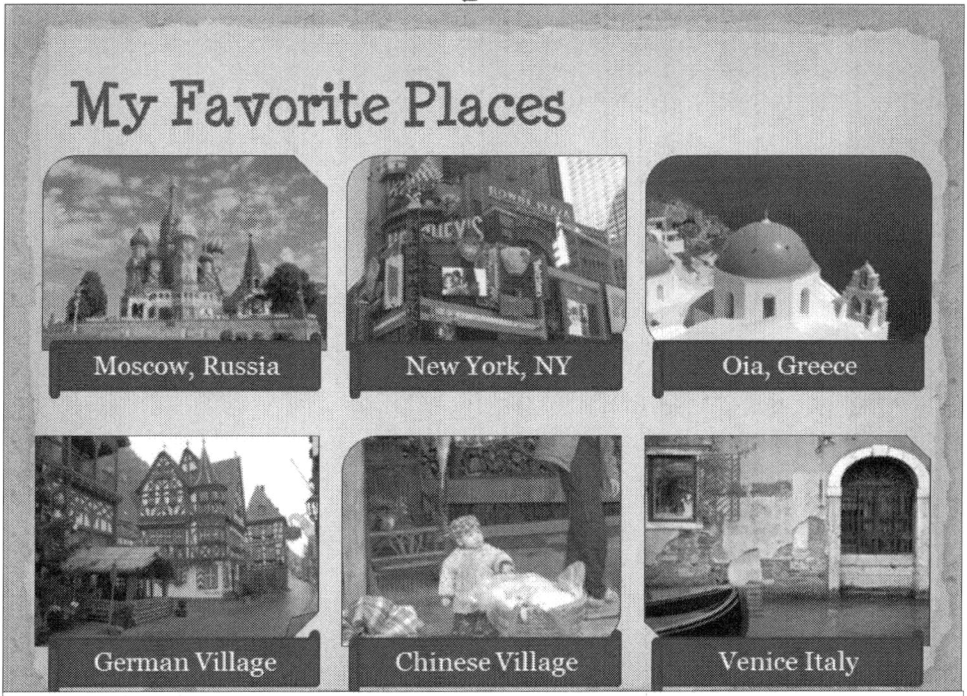

My Favorite Places

Moscow, Russia	New York, NY	Oia, Greece
German Village	Chinese Village	Venice Italy

My Favorite Food

- Indian Food
- Mexican Food
- Chocolate
- Italian Food
- Lobster

Activity Ten

Did You Know?: Did You Know? originally started out as a PowerPoint presentation in August 2006 by Karl Fisch during a faculty meeting at Arapahoe High School in Colorado. The presentation "went viral" on the Web in February 2007. Today, the old and new versions of the online presentation have been seen by millions of people. It is a creative style of producing multimedia presentations that is being used by educators to reach their students. Students are creating such presentations to learn and communicate to larger audiences. It is a great way to reinforce concepts while taking factual information and putting it into a format that is digestible and more engaging. I have shared this curriculum with my colleague. Her students have done their projects on topics such as crazy inventions, the impact of fast food on health, strange facts, food facts, social media statistics, war statistics, eating disorders, the food industry, etc. The topics are limitless. The online unit has links to population, animals, environment, poverty and food.

> When you go to the site, visit the Lesson page that will walk you through steps in order to complete this unit. There are handouts, resources, and examples to assist in this unit.

Animoto Production

 Change Song
Beautiful Being (Lord Running ... - Eastern Sun

Did You Know?
by Chris Clementi

More than 1 billion people don't have access to safe

14 billion pounds of garbage into the ocean every year.

Over 1 million seabirds sea mammals are killed by

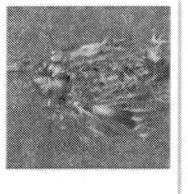

Americans throw away about 28 bottles and jars every year

Recycling just ONE aluminum enough energy to

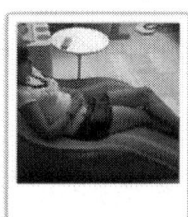

Animoto is an online video maker for consumers, educators and businesses. Animoto makes it easy to create professional, attractive and interesting videos. You can set up a free account for 30 second videos. Check out education options.

32

Animoto Example

Movie Example

"Worldwide, as many as 70,000 deaths occur each year from pregnancy and childbirth for girls aged 15-19."
~Unicef

Google Slide Example

"Every year nearly 900,000,000 trees are cut down to provide raw materials for American paper and pulp mills."

~Epa.gov

Prezi Example

"About a third of women aged 20-24 years old in the developing world were married as children."
~Unicef

Activity Eleven

Alphabet Literacy: I am always trying to come up with creative ways for my students to learn tools while building literacy. Our middle school has recently added an ESL (English as a Second Language) magnet program. I thought it would be such a great idea to have my students create PowerPoints with images and audio to help those students build their vocabulary. My students had a great time putting these presentations together. They thoroughly enjoyed working with a partner on this project. Though partnerships are not necessary for this unit, it adds to the element of collaboration and teamwork. Students that moved further than their partner were more than willing to provide assistance to help their team-mate. Some students figured out ways to be more efficient with their time, deviating somewhat from my method of organization. We invited the ESL students and teacher to come and provide feedback on the presentations. Their constructive criticism was helpful in order to make improvements for future projects and it helped my students understand how they could have used more descriptive sentences to complement the photos they used for their projects. This unit could incorporate basic to advanced language.

Online Alphabet Unit

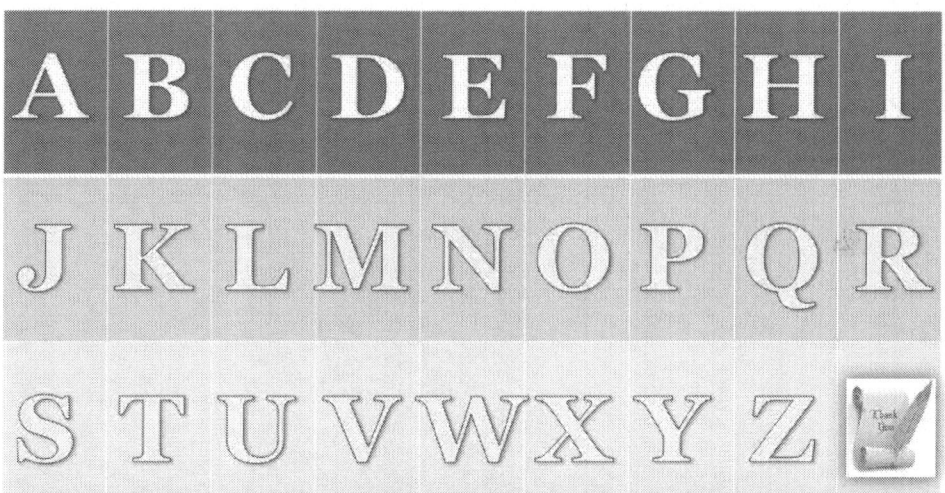

💡 **Slide Template:** The PowerPoint template has been created so students can get a copy and customize it according to the words they are representing for the project. It is set up to link to slides and return home. This can be used to build vocabulary. It could also be used as a tool to teach complicated academic concepts. The following page has some examples of how the slides might look when completed.

Alphabet Literacy

Ex: The students locate all the images to represent the letters of the alphabet. They write and record sentences. Afterwards, they add their voice to the sound icon. The teacher can set up this activity to be as simple or as complicated as they so choose.

R is for Rhino

A female rhino will use her horn to protect her young.

R is for Rhino

The rhino mother must protect her young, who is born without a horn. The mothers tend to be loving and very attentive towards their offspring.

Activity Twelve

Visual Literacy: According to the Merriam Dictionary, Visual Literacy is the ability to recognize and understand ideas conveyed through visible actions or images. According to Johns Hopkins University, "Visual literacy instruction will better prepare students for the dynamic and constantly changing online world they will inevitably be communicating through." Many of my projects require students to locate images that complement language. For example, they have broken down poetry into easily digestible segments. They had to locate images that they thought would complement the words to bring meaning to them and a larger audience. With the combination of words and visuals, they put multimedia presentations together. They have located quotes, idioms, puns, vocabulary words, etc. that they found interesting. Once they had enough language, they had to determine which type of image would reinforce the meaning of the words. Teachers could take this a step further and have the students take their own photos or video to accompany language. One of the units that I had my 7th graders complete involved taking a more complicated word and putting meaning to it through video.

Online Literacy Unit

Visual Literacy

Examples
- Anti Bullying
- Book Covers
- Charities
- Dust Bowl
- Events Quilt-1980s
- Funny Images
- Foreign Language
- Happy Quotes
- History
- Humor
- Idioms
- Internet Safety
- Literacy
- Motivation
- Poetry
- Random Quotes
- Reading Quotes
- Resilience
- States
- U.S. Map
- Vocabulary
- World Problems

Home

Welcome to my session that will focus on visual literacy in the classroom. According to the Merriam Dictionary, visual literacy is the ability to recognize and understand ideas conveyed through visible actions or images. Melissa Thibault and David Walbert define visual literacy as "the ability to see, to understand, and ultimately to think, create, and communicate graphically. According to Monica Martinez, a CEO of a tech company in California, "Technology is changing how we access information and how we communicate it to others…

💡 When you visit the resources page, you will find handouts that require students to locate images and then construct a sentence to complement the visual. There are 15 downloads and descriptions about the activities on this page.

Example

"He that loves reading has everything within his reach." ~William Godwin

This is one of the examples from the Quotes Unit, available to those who purchase this book. Students locate quotes and then must find a large quality image to complement each quote. Students thoroughly enjoy this unit. If this unit is not taught according to the instructional videos, the results tend to be less impressive because students ignore design principles. It is imperative that students respect design tips so that the results are awesome. If you purchase this book, be sure to send an e-mail to kidsnetsoft@gmail.com so I can invite you to the lesson.

Example

Quilt Project This is an example of a quilt project on WW II. Students can put together a visual "quilt" to represent a theme or era. Once they create a visual diagram, they can set up the images to link to sites, videos, audio, etc. Some themes could be about healthy food, events, people, inventions, etc.

Examples

Directions: Fill in the table below. Find 10 images that interest you online. To understand how to add images to AutoShapes, watch the **autoshape tips** video. For every image you add to this table, you must use 10 or more adjectives to describe the photo. You can use the built in thesaurus of Microsoft Word or search online for descriptive words. Afterwards, write two or more sentences describing the image, using three or more of the adjectives from your list. The first one is done as an example.

10 Adjectives	Picture
Old, abandoned, dilapidated, neglected, uninhabited, isolated, historical, interesting, undersized, derelict	
Sentence	
The undersized and dilapidated building was abandoned for unknown reasons. Only the last residents can fully understand why they had to leave this structure vulnerable to the unyielding forces of nature.	

Directions: You want to expand your business and have a shop so you can make additional money off products that promote your business. You are to design the products below and write a description that will make anyone want to buy your product. Don't forget to write down your company's name.

Product	Description
Company Name: Cactus Juice Cafe	
	This 100% cotton shirt, created in the United States, comes in a variety of sizes and colors. It is extremely comfortable and looks great with jeans. Every time you wear this shirt to our restaurant, we will give you a free round of our homemade salsa and chips. If more than one person at your table wears this shirt, our staff will sing you a song or two. For every t-shirt sold, we will give 5% to one of our local charities.
	This 20 ounce can contains our famous spicy cactus jelly. It is made with pure ingredients from local farmers. It is made on the premises of our restaurant. We pride ourselves in serving our customers quality products. We decided to create a spicy cactus jelly for all you chili lovers. We noticed that our customers were adding the jelly to some of their spicy dishes. Once you have finished this delicious jelly, you can use the glass for beverages.

Examples

Literacy Units

Assignments available in Google Docs: Make a copy of each Google Doc and share it with your students. Students can share with their peers and collaborate to solve problems. Click on the image and get the activity.

Google Units: On the site, you can access this interactive Google Drawing. When you click on one of the images, it will force you to make a copy of the Google Doc. Once it is in your Google Drive, you can rename it and share it with students. Be sure to keep the original as a template so you can reuse it.

Activity Thirteen

Get Wise Online: Get Wise Online is a unit I put together to have published in the Ed Tech Magazine. Since its creation, I have modified it extensively for my 8th grade students. Though there are videos on sexting and online safety, the majority of the unit focuses on bullying. During this unit, I tell my students that I don't think bullying will ever go away. Because I firmly believe this, I think it is imperative they have tools and learn coping skills to be able to withstand bullying, should they become victimized. My students always look forward to this unit. Many open up and the other students tend to be very sensitive and understanding. I let the counselor know if students open up so they can be counseled and dealt with accordingly. They need to know their voices are being heard and we care for them. Check out the Alternative Unit. This is the main unit used with 8th graders. They choose groups to come up with tips for teens and then film their tips. They create Animoto presentations with their video. I take the best film from all the groups and put together an Animoto and show it at our All School Assembly each semester. Students can always take photos or locate images online to put this presentation together as an alternative assignment.

Online Get Wise Unit

Get Wise Online
Helping Students be Safe

Navigation
- Home
- Introduction
- The Task
- The Process
- Resources
  - Additional Videos
  - Animoto Example
  - Cover It Live Video
  - How to Videos
  - IB Guidlines
  - Internet Safety Example
  - Netiquette Example
  - PowerPoint Example
- Evaluate
  - NETS for Students
- Author
- Alternative Assignment

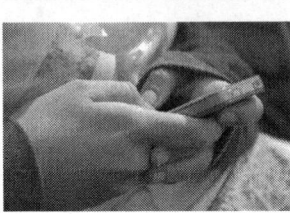

Welcome to a unit on Internet topics that will enlighten anyone that goes online. This unit requires you to go through 5 steps in order to fully appreciate the online culture. As the world continues to embrace the Internet as part of their normal routine, it is imperative that they make good choices and contribute positively to their communities and the world for that matter. Go through the 5 steps below so you can learn about online topics that can help you navigate more easily and have a healthier experience by using some of the tips...

Navigation
- Home
- Introduction
- The Task
- The Process
- Resources
- Evaluate
- Author
- Alternative Assignment
- Sitemap

Students put together an Animoto presentation that should empower viewers as they educate them about how to handle bullies and others concerning online issues. The teacher would like feedback...

Tips Offered by Students

"The weak bully, but the strong help others"

"Talk to someone you trust."   "Block the bully."

"Do you know who you are talking to online?"

"Do things that make you happy"   "Sign Off!"

"Your words are strong, choose wisely."

"Do your words make people smile?" "Get a hobby!"

"Speak up and use your voice."   "Make people smile!"

"Join a club."   "What would your grandma say?"

"Don't be a bystander."   "Save harmful evidence."

"Tell the bully to stop."   "Niceness is priceless."

"Online abuse has an offline impact."

"Turn something negative into something positive?"

"Be an up stander."   "Use strong passwords."

"How is it a joke if I'm not laughing?"

"Bullying can have a lifetime impact." "Be confident!"

"Take a stand, lend a hand."   "Think before sending."

"Apologize if you hurt someone."

Animoto Example

The first image is an example of an Animoto presentation in edit mode. This example consists of teen tips with copyright friendly images. Students in my class actually film 10 second clips to complement the tips. If filming isn't an option, get photos instead.

Online Culture Tips to make this world a	Niceness is priceless.		If the bullying doesn't talk to a trusted adult.	
How is it a joke if I'm not laughing?		Step up so others won't get	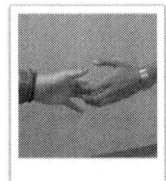	Be confident it tends to keep bullies

YouTube Video

Activity Fourteen

Pixlr Workshop: Pixlr is a free online image editor. I have been teaching Adobe Photoshop to my students since 2003. It is an outstanding image editor; however, not all students can afford to purchase this software. Consequently, I became relatively proficient with using Pixlr so I can give my students an alternative tool should they choose to explore on their own at home or get caught up on classroom projects. Students will go home and work on this project if they fall behind or want to go above and beyond. The final products end up being very impressive. I was truly amazed with one of my students who explored the tools beyond my videos. She came up with very creative products. With so much emphasis on visual presentations, it is a skill that could easily come in handy for students. Students might want to become better photo editors for personal reasons or they may choose a career in photo editing. This skill will come in handy when creating multimedia presentations, developing websites for school or work, creating a resume that stands out from others, etc. It is not just fun to edit photos, it can actually pay off for a variety of reasons. If time is an issue or students need modified curriculum, be sure to check out the modified options link.

Online Pixlr Unit

KidsnetSoft Pixlr

- **Home**
- Agenda
- Efficient
- Gallery
- Instructor
- Multi-media
- Products
- ▼ Videos
  - Animals Part 1
  - Animals Part 2
  - Banners
  - Blemishes
  - Blurry
  - Desaturate
  - Eye Color
  - Hair Color
  - Magic
  - Makeup
  - Red Eye
  - Tattoos
  - Twin Effect

Home

Welcome to Kidsnetsoft's Pixlr Workshop. Pixlr is a great alternative to the expensive software. Consequently, I have decided to make several lessons using this fabulous online tool. Students can go home and work on projects for free. They can become masters of the software if they so choose. The beauty of learning Pixlr is that you can transfer some of that knowledge to other software...

Manipulating Images

| Home | Example | Images | Thanks | Videos |

Home

Click on the Modified Options link to get image combinations ready for students to download and manipulate. How to videos are also available on this site.

Pixlr Examples

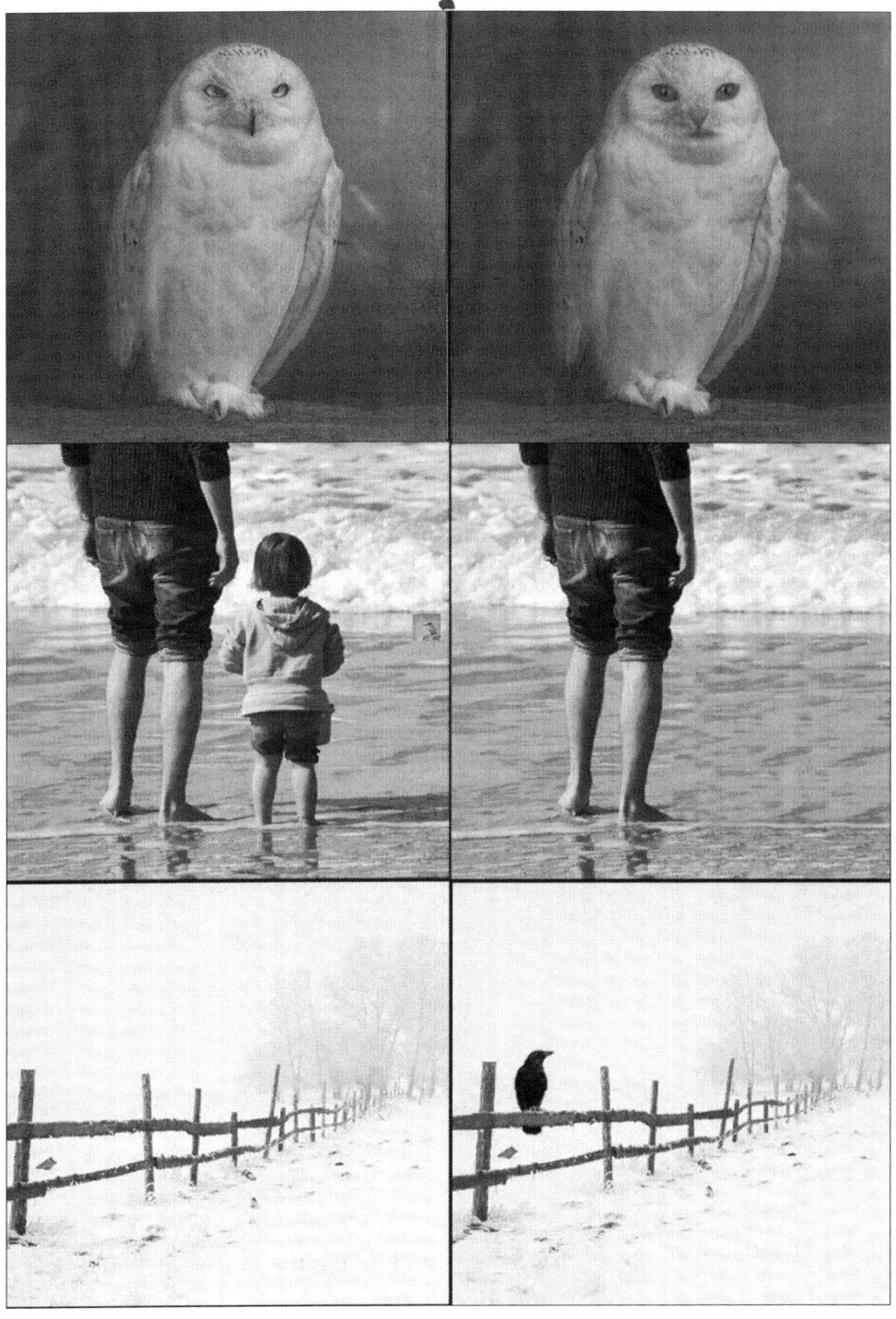

Pixlr Examples

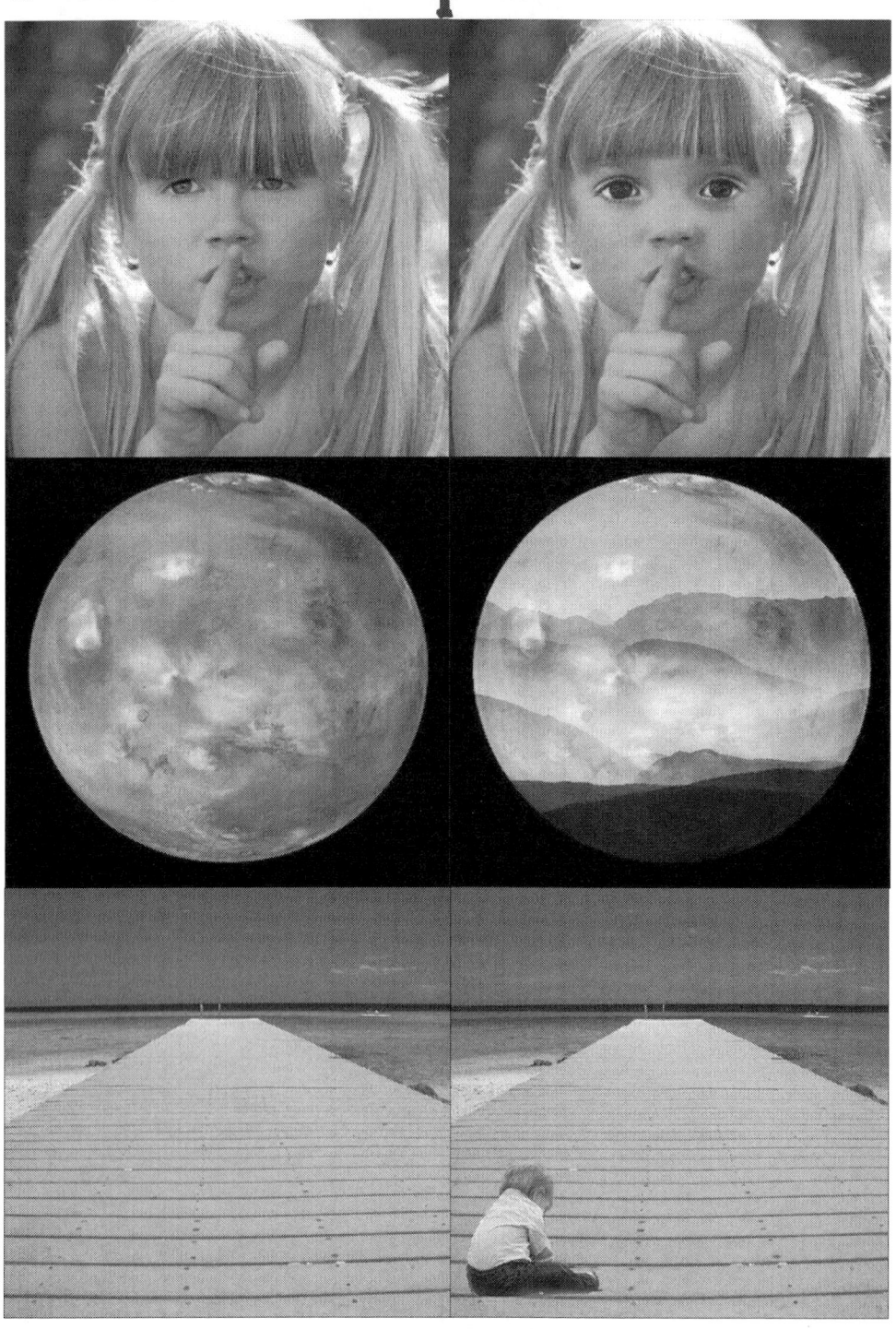

Activity Fifteen

Fable Unit: I got the idea to create this unit after attending a workshop in creative writing. I thought it would be fabulous to have students find a fable and re-write it. I am always coming up with great ideas but often don't have time to incorporate it into my already tight curriculum. This unit would be fabulous for a Language Arts class. I decided to share this unit with our other computer design teacher and she gladly incorporated the lesson into her curriculum. She modified it by having the students re-write the fable for modern times, using more current jargon and situations. She then had them gather images to accompany the re-written story and then add their voices to create a multimedia presentation to their story. A teacher can take this unit and easily customize it to the needs of their students and content. The unit requires students to record their voices using a free online audio editor called Audacity. If recording their voice is not an option, they can break down the script into digestible parts and then add images to complement the words. Students can use such free online tools as Powtoons, Photo Peach, Moovly, WeVideo, Stupeflix, etc. Google "free online movie makers" to get more ideas. These tools seem to pop up constantly. It is truly difficult to keep up.

Online Fable Unit

KidsnetSoft Fable Unit

| Home | Lesson | Audacity | Example | Thanks | Videos |

Welcome to the fun and exciting unit on Fables. This unit will allow participants to create an audio story after they re-write a fable of choice. When re-writing the story, the students should embellish the original story, adding more adjectives, adverbs, complex sentences, etc. They can even change the moral of the story if they so choose. Once they re-write the fable, they will record their voices in Audacity. They are welcome to change their voices, however, don't change it so much that we don't understand the story. When the story has been recorded, students can gather the visuals to complement the story and then put it together with a variety of multi-media tools.

Original Story of The Boys and the Frogs

"Some mischievous boys were playing on the edge of a pond, and, catching sight of some Frogs swimming about in the shallow water, they began to amuse themselves by pelting them with stones, and they killed several of them. At last one of the Frogs put his head out of the water and said, "Oh, stop! stop! I beg of you! What is sport to you is death to us."

Revised Fable

The Boys and the Frogs: Summers in rural Illinois can be quite harrowing for some critters. It was a hot July day when some mischievous and very unruly boys were playing on the edge of a pond, deep in the forest where they would often go to get away from their parents or siblings. To the disadvantage of the indigenous frogs who resided in the pond, these boys had a plan that would disturb anyone with a conscience. Each boy looked at each other with a wicked grin, as if they knew what each other was thinking. Within seconds of their grins, they grabbed a handful of stones and began assaulting them with their ammunition, as if they were at an amusement park trying to win a stuffed animal. The results of their barbaric act resulted in the death of several defenseless and harmless frogs. Finally, one of the frightened and exhausted frogs put his head out of the water and said, "Oh, stop! stop! I beg of you: what is sport to you is death to us." To the frog's dismay, the boys lacking the sensitivity and values of their peers, continued to pelt them until each frog had perished. When the boys ran home, they came across Ralph and his hooligan friends. The events that took place after that are too disturbing to re-tell. I guess the moral of the story would be "what goes around comes around."

Activity Sixteen

Digital Footprint: "On the Internet a digital footprint is the word used to describe the trail, traces or "footprints" that people leave online. This is information transmitted online, such as forum registration, e-mails and attachments, uploading videos or digital images and any other form of transmission of information — all of which leaves traces of personal information about yourself available to others online." Every time you go online, you leave a footprint. What you post can be searched by anyone. It can be copied, shared, and permanent. With over 2 billion people using the Internet, it is important to leave a digital footprint that is positive and beneficial to the world. Current and potential employers are looking at your social media pages to determine if you are an applicant they can trust to represent their company or institution. Employers can search and see if your name pops up. Social media sites like Facebook, Twitter, and LinkedIn are highly searchable. This gives recruiters the opportunity to form an opinion without ever meeting you. Because the stakes can be so high with impacting a person's reputation, preventing employment, getting fired, etc. it is imperative students become informed to stay safe and protect their reputation.

Online Footprints Unit

Online Footprints' Unit

| Home | Prints | Quotes | Resources | Tips | Videos |

The Internet is a fantastic resource that can help many with finding decent employment. According to Undercover Recruiter, if you have no social media presence, it can indicate to prospective employers that you are inept when it comes to the Internet. They say at minimum, one should have a robust profile on Linkedin. Many employers would prefer candidates have savvy and active Facebook and Twitter profiles. "According to Forbes, two of the key personality traits employers look for are intellectual curiosity and self-monitoring. Nearly 60% of employers are looking for these traits that are readily demonstrated by a discerning social media presence." Of course this depends on what kind of employment you are seeking. Considering an online profile can become an asset for some professionals, it is imperative that it is created thoughtfully and responsibly. Though we want to discourage our students from posting their names online, it isn't too early to educate them about posting responsibly. They need to ask the following questions before posting: Is the information true?...

Footprint Quotes

"You are what you share." ~C.W. Leadbeater

"Great brands listen, learn and then leverage" ~Bernard Kelvin Clive

"If you don't define yourself online, someone else will." ~Rebekah Radice

"I can't control who follows me, but I can control who I follow. [Social Media]" ~Germany Kent

"Say something worthwhile and people will listen." ~Germany Kent

"Lifting lives, 140 characters at a time." ~Germany Kent

"Life should be like a good Tweet - short, pithy, convey a message and inspire others to follow." ~Ashok Kallarakkal

"Pay it forward with free compliments. They are returned in due time." ~NetworkEtiquette.net"

"Search engines finds the information, not necessarily the truth." ~Amit Kalantri

"Thou shalt not use the 140 characters limit as an excuse for bad grammar and/or incorrect spelling." ~Mokokoma Mokhonoana

"Think of the Internet as a public place. Don't leave your details lying around" ~Postgraduate student

Actual Footprints

"A California Pizza Kitchen worker was fired for his tweeting. His profanity on the company's Twitter page, along with his strong negative opinions about the company's new uniforms, led to his dismissal. "

"A Denver math teacher published revealing photos on her social media account and tweeted about pot smoking and other behaviors that we would not think of as characteristic of a teacher. These posts got her fired in spite of popularity among her students."

"A Seattle coffee shop fired a barista who started a blog about the daily tribulations of his job…He even poked fun at his boss, writing, "I like to use a lot of big words when I tweet, that way if my boss ever finds my twitter account, he won't understand any of it.""

"Elizabeth Lauten, communications director for Republican Rep. Fincher, was asked to resign after making the following comments about the children of President Obama. ""Dear Sasha and Malia, I get you're both in those awful teen years, but you're a part of the First Family, try showing a little class. At least respect the part you play. Then again your mother and father don't respect their positions very much, or the nation for that matter, so I'm guessing you're coming up a little short in the 'good role model' department. Nevertheless, stretch yourself. Rise to the occasion. Act like being in the White House matters to you. Dress like you deserve respect, not a spot at a bar.""

Actual Footprints

"After the wake of a disastrous tsunami that claimed numerous lives and devastated coastal towns in Japan, comic Gilbert Gottfried, the voice of the Aflac duck, got fired after tweeted several off-color jokes. This is one example of his jokes: "Japan is really advanced. They don't go to the beach. The beach comes to them."

"A waitress became irritated after she had to stay past her shift to wait on a table of two. When the customers finally departed, they left what the waitress deemed an inadequate tip. "Thanks for eating at Brixx," she reportedly wrote on her Facebook page, before using profanity and calling the customers "cheap.""

"Adam Smith, former CEO, lost his job and had to go on food stamps after he videotaped himself telling the drive-thru attendant how much he despised Chick-Fil-A. Once he posted the video, it went viral and he found himself unemployed."

A director of a corporation began tweeting during her travel to South Africa. She tweeted the following on her departure flight: "Weird German Dude: You're in First Class. It's 2014. Get some deodorant." On her flight to Cape Town, she tweeted: "Going to Africa. Hope I don't get AIDS. Just kidding. I'm white!"

"A Bloomberg social media editor lost his job this spring after a Twitter contact shared a private direct message he had sent about frustrations at work."

Actual Footprints

The day after a sixth grader from Harlem drowned in the Atlantic Ocean on a class outing, Ms. Rubino, a teacher from Brooklyn, was given a two-year suspension without pay after her comments on Facebook. She posted "after today, I am thinking the beach sounds like a wonderful idea for my 5th graders? I HATE THEIR GUTS! They are all the devils spawn!" She added, concerning one student, "I would not throw a life jacket in for a million."

"A British teen was let go from a marketing gig after colleagues saw a Facebook post in which she described her job shredding paper as "dull," even though she didn't mention the name of the company."

"A teacher in Georgia was asked to resign because of a Facebook photo of her holding wine and a beer."

"A city clerk in California's Bay area was asked to resign this year for allegedly tweeting during council meetings when she was supposed to be taking down meeting minutes."

"Two probationary teachers faced termination for their Facebook musings that "I'm feeling pissed because I hate my students," and I'm "teaching in the most ghetto school in Charlotte."

 "A whopping 93% of recruiters check out social media profiles of prospective hires." Time.com

Activity Seventeen

Chrome Apps and Extensions: Every chance I get, I attend the Google for Education Summit in Colorado. It gives me a chance to learn many creative and innovative uses for Google tools so that I can continue to improve my teaching. I was very excited to attend a session that shares some of Google Chrome's Apps and Extensions. I put together a visually attractive chart that highlights some of the more popular Apps and Extensions. Each image has a link to the site where you can download the App or Extension and then there is a link to a helpful video that either highlight its capabilities or demonstrates how to use it. This chart will remain current and I invite you to let me know if one is no longer available or if you think an App or Extension should be added to the chart. Whenever I come across some interesting Apps or Extensions, I add it to this chart. It will continue to be useful with continual research and feedback from you.

> When you visit Activity #17 on the website, you can download a useful handout at the bottom of the page. You can have teachers complete this for a workshop or use it for personal reference.

Apps & Extensions

The video icon will link to an instructional video while the home icon links to the download page.

Activity Eighteen

Google Drawings: After attending the Google for Education Summit in Colorado in 2014, I learned about some fabulous ways to incorporate Google Drawings into my activities. I left that session enormously impressed and elated. I immediately went home and changed a unit I have been doing with my students since 2004. I know it is wise to change up lessons more frequently than that, but this unit is a fabulous unit. Students completed a poster on endangered animals using Microsoft Word. They not only learned some fabulous tools in Microsoft Word, but they learned about design, facts about animals and their writing skills are reinforced during this unit. By changing it to Google Drawings, students are able to make the poster much more dynamic. They locate sounds and videos and make links on their poster so viewers could hear the sounds and watch educational or fun videos about the animals represented on their posters. Students that get ahead can record their information in Audacity, a free sound editor, and then make links for viewers to hear their words. Students are invited to a Google site to add their posters. Each student provides constructive feedback to at least 3 of their peers so that improvements can be made. You can get many ideas by clicking on the Example link of the online unit.

Online Drawings' Unit

Online Drawings' Unit

| Home | Agenda | Examples | Product | US Map | Videos |

Google Drive has so many fabulous opportunities for education. As a computer teacher, I try to provide literacy and tech-rich opportunities for my students. After attending the Colorado Summit featuring Google Education, I learned about some fabulous ways to incorporate Google Drawings into my activities. This site showcases some interesting ways you can use Google Drawings in education. One of my favorite examples will include a poster on endangered animals. I have been doing this unit using Microsoft Word for years. It is a great unit because students learn facts about animals, note taking, improving writing skills, learning tools and learning about design. Before attending the Summit, I had no idea I could actually end up with a product that is more dynamic. Though Microsoft Word might have more extensive tools than Google Drawings, I think there are more creative opportunities with Google.

See Activity #7 for more details about the Poster Unit. That unit emphasizes reading, writing, design, creativity and organization.

Drawing Examples

Elbot: Type in questions or comments and Elbot will respond!

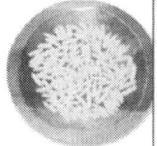

Freerice: Answer multiple choice questions about a variety of topics. Each time you answer correctly, 10 grains of rice is donated to the United Nations World Food Program.

Linerider: Draw paths and scenery and hit play to see the bobber move. It taps into creativity and trial and error.

Monkey e-mail: Send a monkey e-mail with a message consisting of your voice or a computerized voice.

Apples: The **apples** were beautiful to look at and definitely tasty and nutritious to eat.

Angry: The spoiled boy became very **angry** when he didn't get his way.

Artist: The **artist** made his living by drawing cartoon characters of people.

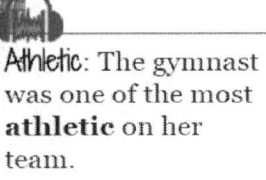

Athletic: The gymnast was one of the most **athletic** on her team.

Alligator: The **alligator** looked mean and ferocious with his sharp teeth.

Site Expectations

 Google Calendar: You need to create an event for each month.	Animoto needs at least 25 images or video and at least 6 titles related to site. 	 A 300 word write-up with a picture to go with the content.	At least 4 cropped images with a 60 word write-up per image.	Gallery Page: 12 cropped images		
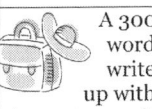 A 300 word write-up with a picture to go with the content.	At least 4 cropped images with a 60 word write-up per image.	Gallery Page: 12 cropped images 	Animoto needs at least 25 images or video and at least 6 titles related to site.	A publisher product turned into an image like a calendar or menu.		
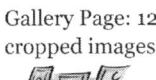 A Google form asking at least 8 questions related to site.	Gallery Page: 12 cropped images 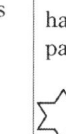	Everyone must have a home page.	A Q/A page that has a total of 300 or more words. 	A home-made movie about 1 minute long related to site.		
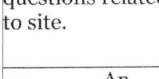 An image map that will have at least 8 different hyperlinks.	A home-made movie about 1 minute long related to site.	Animoto needs at least 25 images or video and at least 6 titles related to site. 	A 300 word write-up with a picture to go with the content.	At least 4 cropped images with a 60 word write-up per image. 	Gallery Page: 12 cropped images	
Gallery Page: 12 cropped images 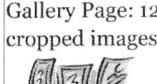	A publisher product turned into an image like a calendar or menu.	A 300 word write-up with a picture to go with the content.	At least 4 cropped images with a 60 word write-up per image.	Come up with an alternative option. Get approval from the teacher 		

This interactive diagram will link to examples of pages 8th graders can create for the website unit. Students use this to help determine what they will create. Each student is responsible for building 5 or more pages each. By providing this interactive diagram, there is less confusion about expectations for the unit.

US Map Unit

United States Map: Teachers and students can download a map template that has each state set up to link to a variety of possible products. My goal is to have each state link to a possible project idea. Some of the states link to educational sites, Animoto, Powtoons, Google Slides, Thinglink, Glogster, Quizlet, Tour Builder, a Google Map and EdPuzzle. The potential for this project are endless. To get to the map example, follow this path: Google Drawings Unit/ Us Map tab/ map example link. You can scroll over various states to see the examples. There are resources, handouts, and ideas available for this unit if you choose to implement it in class. Teachers could assign each student a state and set up links to their work.

Activity Nineteen

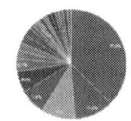

Google Surveys: This unit has so much fabulous potential. I try to incorporate as many Google tools as possible. I decided to have my 8th graders make a Google survey. I didn't put much thought into the lesson. I gave them a few expectations without providing some guidance and a rubric. The results were literally catastrophic. Most of them asked terrible questions. For example, one student asked silly questions and didn't give them an out. He asked a checkbox question which allows more than one option. The set-up went something along these lines: Which statements are true? a) Joe (fictitious name of actual student) is incredibly brilliant b) Joe is gorgeous c) Joe is the best d) I love Joe. The question was mandatory. So imagine a student not liking any of these options. The student did not have an "Other option. Afterwards, I put together a unit that required them to look at helpful videos and I came up with a well-thought-out rubric. I researched what makes a good survey so that I could incorporate that into my rubric. If you visit the Agenda page, you can walk your students through the process. Adjust it as you see fit for your class. After students made their survey, students took the surveys of assigned peers and provided constructive feedback. They e-mailed those students informing them how to improve their surveys if necessary.

Online Survey Unit

Online Survey Unit

| Home | Agenda | Examples | Ideas | Rubric | Videos |

Welcome to the making surveys site. This site should help students have a better foundation before they create surveys in order to gather data. In the past, I had my students make surveys without giving them tips or some kind of focus and the outcomes were atrocious. They would make surveys that others refused to complete because they were written poorly. Some didn't have a focus. They had mandatory questions that didn't give the user an out. For example, one student asked what is your favorite sport and the options were baseball, football, basketball and hockey. The problem with such a question is the user might not like any of those sports. They should have added an other category to give the user an out. When you visit the Agenda page, you can complete the tasks in order to learn best practices when constructing a survey. The Resources page will have more information if you want to learn about surveys in further depth.

"Keep it simple. No one wants to take a lengthy survey, so pick one key issue to focus on and ask 5-10 questions about it." ~Rieva Lesonsky

Activity Twenty

Presentation Jeopardy: I have done a Jeopardy activity with my students using Microsoft PowerPoint. The students had a great time working on this project in groups of 2-3. I decided to create a Presentation in Google. Anyone can pick up the template and use it for their classroom. Teachers can save the original as a template and then share it with their students via Google Classroom. Otherwise, teachers can pick one student from a small group to pick it up in Google templates and then share it with their assigned partners in Google Drive. The teacher can have students download the plan on the site to be edited in Microsoft Word or they can have students download the template in Google Docs. I think the most exciting way to complete this assignment is to have one student pick up the templates in Google Templates and then share them with their partners. Students really enjoy having their peers editing projects at the same time. Students can decide who sets up which category. They can then help their partners if they are falling behind. I have done similar projects with collaboration and the students really step up. The site has instructions to assist in picking up the materials.

Jeopardy Template

Click on a level question

Category 1	Category 2	Category 3	Category 4	Category 5
100	100	100	100	100
200	200	200	200	200
300	300	300	300	300
400	400	400	400	400
500	500	500	500	500

Jeopardy Plan

Category 1		
Level	Question	Answer
100		
200		
300		
400		
500		

Category 2		
Level	Question	Answer
100		
200		
300		
400		

Activity Twenty One

Google Sites: When I started teaching middle school computer design in 2003, I had my students make websites in Microsoft Word. I wanted them to improve their organization skills, respect copyright laws, and learn what makes a good website. It was definitely not the most ideal tool to use, but we made it work. After becoming a Google Certified Teacher, I learned more about the power of Google. Google Sites has evolved into a fabulous tool. I can only imagine it will continue to improve. I embraced it as a platform for my 8th graders to make extensive sites on a hypothetical country, museum or business. They can choose to do an alternative website. For instance, one of my students went to India during this unit and he put together an informational site about India. He added facts, experiences, and personal photos. This unit taps into their creativity on so many levels. I continue to modify this lesson. Students are able to add surveys, videos, Google Drawings, Google Presentations, Google Calendars, image galleries, etc. They learn what makes a good website should they choose to continue on the path of Web Design. I had a student become so passionate about Web Design that she reconsidered her desire to be a Veterinarian. Maybe she can make the website for her veterinarian clinic.

Google Sites Unit

Google Sites Unit

Home
▼ **Agenda**
   Examples
   Plan
   Getting Started
   Collaborating
   Color Scheme
   Background
   Banner 1
   Banner 2
   Homepage
   Adding Tables
   Adding Images
   Links
  ▶ Adding Sound
   Video
   Forms
   Horizontal
   Attachments
   Hot Spots
Images
Presenter
Products
Resources
Thanks

This site has been set up to provide great tips on web-site building using Google Sites. You will be able to create sites and banners from scratch. You can learn how to add images, tables, sound, video and much more. This online session will also demonstrate how to create a Google Form and then embed it on your website. Google Sites are a great way to communicate with your students, parents and staff. Make your students' lives easier by having a site they can go for resources so they can be successful in your classroom. Provide communication opportunities for parents who might want to know what their kids are doing...

I have shared this unit at the Google for Education Summits in Colorado. It is packed with helpful resources to get one started on making attractive and functional Google Sites. Feel free to e-mail me if a resource needs updating. kidsnetsoft@gmail.com

Website Examples

The Island of Guaca

- Home
- Art
- ▶ Attractions
- Calendar
- Comments
- Culture
- Disclaimer
- Events
- Feedback
- Film School
- History
- ▶ Hotels
- Map
- QA
- Resources
- Shopping
- Sounds
- Thanks
- Tourists
- Sitemap

Home

YouTube Video

Welcome to the official website of the Island of Guaca. Guaca is a small country island who gained independence from the British in the 1800s. Though this island is a little larger than the state of New York, it has a lot to offer its visitors. People travel from all over the world to experience the oddities and wonders of this land. There are many splendid attractions that range from lush forests to sandy beaches. If you visit the attraction's page, you will be able to see a variety of photos. The attraction's page is broken down into galleries dealing with nature, food, music, architecture, animals and museums. A personal favorite of many visitors tends to be the elaborate and exotic foods served throughout the island. You can view some of their famous dishes by clicking on the food section of the attraction's page. Our citizens take great pride in serving food that is delicious and unique. If you scroll over some of the music images on the music page, you can hear a sample of what the instruments sound like. The animal section will elicit curiosity from anyone. These animals can be found nowhere else in the world. They can be seen in different parts of the wilderness regions of the island. Don't forget to visit our

The Island of Guaca

- Home
- Art
- ▶ Attractions
- Calendar
- Comments
- Culture
- Disclaimer
- Events
- Feedback
- Film School
- History
- ▶ Hotels
- Map
- QA
- Resources
- Shopping
- Sounds
- Thanks
- Tourists
- Sitemap

QA

Get important answers by reading frequently asked questions:

Question: Where would you recommend we go if we are traveling with small children?
Answer: We strongly recommend you go to the Village of Youth. They have an amusement park, parks with modern playground equipment and restaurants that cater to younger visitors.

Question: Are there dangerous places on the Island of Guaca?
Answer: We pride ourselves in the fact that we have the lowest crime rates in the world. You are safe to travel anywhere on our Island. Our people are very happy because we have low unemployment and a very strong sense of community.

Question: If I am traveling in December, do I need to pack warm clothes?
Answer: Because we are along the equator, our temperatures are consistently warm throughout the year. You will want to dress for temperatures ranging from 48 to 70 degrees F in higher altitudes. Coastal areas are consistently warmer ranging from 70-88 degrees F. These temperatures are consistent throughout the year.

Website Examples

Website Examples

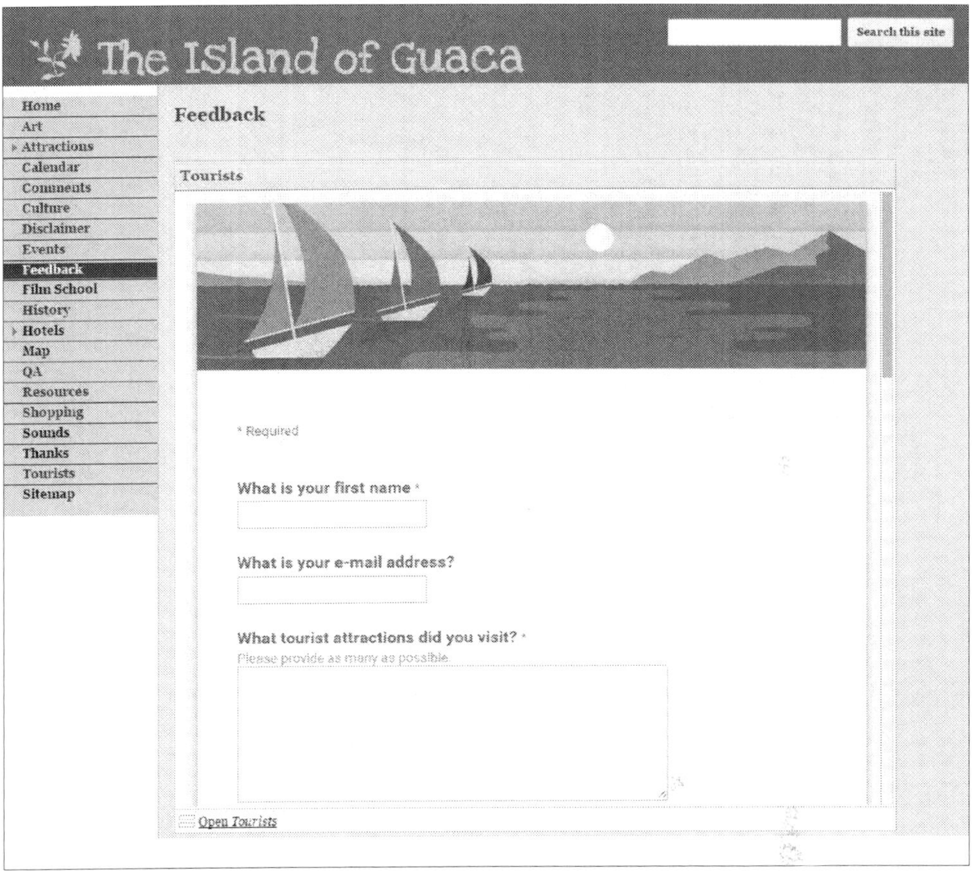

The Island of Guaca

Home
Art
▸ Attractions
Calendar
Comments
Culture
Disclaimer
Events
Feedback
Film School
History
▸ Hotels
Map
QA
Resources
Shopping
Sounds
Thanks
Tourists
Sitemap

Feedback

Tourists

* Required

What is your first name *

What is your e-mail address?

What tourist attractions did you visit? *
Please provide as many as possible

Open *Tourists*

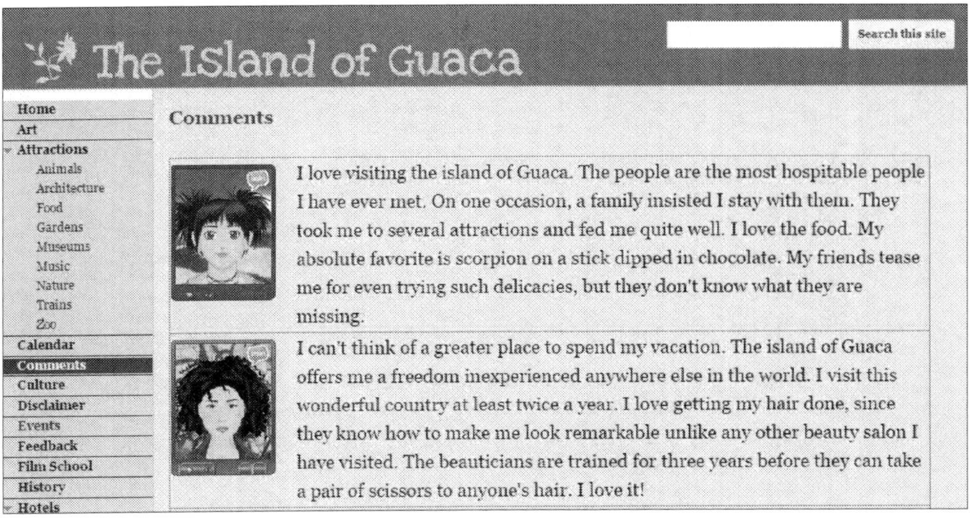

The Island of Guaca

Home
Art
▾ Attractions
  Animals
  Architecture
  Food
  Gardens
  Museums
  Music
  Nature
  Trains
  Zoo
Calendar
Comments
Culture
Disclaimer
Events
Feedback
Film School
History
▾ Hotels

Comments

 I love visiting the island of Guaca. The people are the most hospitable people I have ever met. On one occasion, a family insisted I stay with them. They took me to several attractions and fed me quite well. I love the food. My absolute favorite is scorpion on a stick dipped in chocolate. My friends tease me for even trying such delicacies, but they don't know what they are missing.

 I can't think of a greater place to spend my vacation. The island of Guaca offers me a freedom inexperienced anywhere else in the world. I visit this wonderful country at least twice a year. I love getting my hair done, since they know how to make me look remarkable unlike any other beauty salon I have visited. The beauticians are trained for three years before they can take a pair of scissors to anyone's hair. I love it!

Activity Twenty Two

Google Classroom: Google Classroom has revolutionized the way I teach. Hopefully you can persuade your district to get on board with Google Classroom if they haven't already. Google Classroom allows the teacher to create lessons in Google Drive and then share them with students. It can be set up that students can view a file, edit a file or receive a file in their own Google Drive for editing. Teachers can easily share lessons, attachments, videos, etc. in Google Classroom. I taught this unit to staff members and they were thrilled once they realized the teaching potential. When I introduced it to my students, they were excited to see that I could easily access their work and provide comments. I have transferred the majority of my lessons to Google Drive so that I can share the lessons via Google Classroom. I have a very helpful video on the book site that will walk you through setting up and using Google Classroom. You can access the Workshop page of my site to get some actual activities that I shared with staff members so they could see how Classroom works. They picked up lessons and worked on them while I demonstrated how I could provide feedback simultaneously while they work.

Online Classroom Unit

Google Classroom

| Home | Activities | Example | Resources | Workshop |

Google Classroom has revolutionized my class. Once you set up a class as the teacher, you will get a code that students can use to access your assignments. You can create an assignment in Google Docs, Presentations, or Drawings and push that assignment off to all your students with a few clicks. You can post videos, pdfs, documents, etc. for students to access. Students will then have the material in their Google Drive to edit. You can access your drive and see what students are doing. You can add a comment for the student so they can continue to perfect their work. Once the student acknowledges your comment and takes action, they can click on the resolve button. This session will invite you to some activities...

💡 If your school is not on board with Google Classroom, there are ways to still utilize Google tools to benefit your students. You can always create templates for your students and make them available on the Google templates resource page. You can have students share their work with you.

Sample Lesson

Directions: Add 10 or more adjectives to the story to make it more interesting.

The Æsop for Children: "Belling the Cat"

The Mice once called a meeting to decide on a plan to free themselves of their enemy, the Cat. At least they wished to find some way of knowing when she was coming, so they might have time to run away. Indeed, something had to be done, for they lived in such constant fear of her claws that they hardly dared stir from their dens by night or day.

Many plans were discussed, but none of them was thought good enough. At last a very young Mouse got up and said:

"I have a plan that seems very simple, but I know it will be successful.

All we have to do is to hang a bell about the Cat's neck. When we hear the bell ringing we will know immediately that our enemy is coming."

All the Mice were much surprised that they had not thought of such a plan before. But in the midst of the rejoicing over their good fortune, an old Mouse arose and said:

"I will say that the plan of the young Mouse is very good. But let me ask one question: Who will bell the Cat?"

Sample Lessons
Adding Captions

Replace this text with your caption

Keyword Searches

Directions: Find answers using the Find Function and appropriate keyword searches.

Question	Keyword	Answer
How long can a platypus remain submerged underwater when trying to find food?		
How many adult humans could be killed from the toxin of a pufferfish?		

Activity Twenty Three

Satire: Though I have not taught this unit with my middle school students, I see the power of satire in units, especially in high school. I got the idea to put this unit together after watching a funny video titled "Said No Teacher Ever" by FBC Loganville. I show this to my middle school students and they didn't fully get some of the humor. After showing it to my daughter, who recently graduated from high school, she had a smile on her face for the majority of the video. Teachers, for the most part, appreciate the video. Humor is essential for learning in education. "Humor can be used to simplify, relax, illustrate, and motivate students." Because satire can easily offend audiences, it is important that the unit is well planned. A rules page exists on the online unit to prevent audiences from becoming offended. If they are offended, they will most likely shut down and learning will not occur. "Well-written satire will not only entertain, it will also cause the audience to consider problems that they otherwise might not have been aware of, and may inspire them to actively seek changes that can answer these problems."

> ""The Onion," the satirical news site, can often times be mean-spirited and in bad taste. But sometimes it can sure be funny, too!" Larry Ferlazzo, an award winning English teacher.

Online Satire Unit

Satire Unit

| Home | Examples | Lesson | Resources | Rules | Videos |

Satire defined: "The use of humor, irony, exaggeration, or ridicule to expose and criticize people's stupidity or vices, particularly in the context of contemporary politics and other topical issues." Satire is a creative way for educators to bring awareness to world issues and concerns. Since sarcasm is an attribute of satire, it is important to provide guidelines in this unit. Some topics can be too sensitive and tragic for students to handle. It is important to choose topics that won't cause your students to lose sleep or become overly depressed because the topic struck a nerve. Possible topics that should be brought to the attention of students will be provided on the Topics page. The lesson might require students to research problems of the world, which can be very depressing. I showed my students a presentation I created about what I considered problems of the world and they thought it was a bit gloomy. It is important that students are aware of problems. I don't think students should be sheltered from problems. Hopefully we can give them the tools to be problem solvers. If they are aware of problems, they can become the solution.

"Satire uses humor to highlight problems with the hope that they will be improved upon. " ~Custom Papers

Satirical sites continue to pop up all over the Internet. We need to be cognizant of this so we don't spread irony and sarcasm as truth.

These satirical sites mimic "real" sites leading to the spreading of misinformation across the web. Research and read the disclaimers!

"One of the most popular kinds of humor amongst teenage writers is satire. Satire is a literary form that uses sarcasm and sharp wit to attack something the author deems foolish." ~Scholastic

"Satires are usually playful in form and tone. But don't be deceived! Satires are anything but playful in the end. Behind satirical humor resides a strong political conviction or belief. Satire makes a specific point by attacking its subject with humor." ~Scholastic

"Make a list of political or social issues about which you feel strongly. Choose your subject and attack it with humor." ~Scholastic

"Satire is traditionally the weapon of the powerless against the powerful. I only aim at the powerful. When satire is aimed at the powerless, it is not only cruel — it's vulgar." ~Molly Ivins

Activity Twenty Four

Video Resumes: I got the idea to put this unit together when I heard that some universities and employers are requiring applicants submit a video resume. I researched Youtube to get an idea about some of the video resumes that have been created. I was truly amazed at how incredible some of the videos were and also not so impressed with other examples. I decided to put a resource site together for teachers to use for their classroom. I have 16 examples of video resumes on the site. There is a handout for students to use for reflection. Interestingly enough, after watching video example #9, I sent an e-mail to the creator and asked him if his video got him interviews. He said it did and that he got two job offers. The video is very creative and funny. I would imagine employers that are seeking creative candidates with a fun personality would be eager to hire him. However, more serious companies might want a more serious video. Students could have an interesting dialogue about each video and discuss what company they think might be interested in the candidates based on the video. They could also discuss how they would do it differently. Hopefully watching these videos will spark ideas for students to create their own videos.

Online Video Resume

Online Video Resume Unit

| Home | Assignment | Example | Resources | Tips |

Home

Welcome to the Video Resume Unit. Considering some Universities and employers require candidates to send video resumes and some candidates have created them to stand out in the interview process, I put together this unit to help students create video resumes. Students should have a great time planning and creating their video resumes. It will give them the opportunity to shine if done correctly. Visit the Assignments page so that you can get started on this unit.

According to some schools of thought, if you apply for a usual job in an ordinary office, you don't need to bother with creating a video resume. However, if your position requires creativity, a video resume might be the solution. This site is for those who are seeking employment that requires video resumes or if it will give you an edge in the market. It is also a great addition to your online portfolio.

Video Examples

***Directions:** Watch each video and reflect on the document titled video reflection.

Example 1: Video resume for Pizza Hut.
Example 2: This actor is humorous. Is this a good or bad thing?
Example 3: Setting up video resumes for specific jobs.
Example 4: Innovation and Product Management
Example 5: This is a serious video resume worth checking out.
Example 6: "A Cavalcade of Crappy video resumes."
Example 7: Dhaval VCV video resume
Example 8: Professional Video Resume with Niala
Example 9: Eric Purdue Video Resume
Example 10: The Funniest Video Resume Ever
Example 11: Rachell Flores' Video Resume
Example 12: Christine Kiernan's Video Resume
Example 13: Samanth Little's Video Resume
Example 14: Rendered in Adobe Photoshop and After Effects.
Example 15: Crysta Timmerman's Video Resume
Example 16: Un QR Code by Maxime Delmas

Extra Sites

Extra Sites: This page will continue to expand as I come across interesting sites for the classroom or just for fun. Students will bring fabulous sites to my attention and I will add it to the site. My students might have a couple of minutes before class ends and choose to visit this resource page if they are caught up in class. They enjoy visiting these links because they are engaging and fun. Many will go home and continue visiting these resources as a means of educational entertainment. Many will tap into their creativity. Elbot is a popular site that allows students to have a conversation with a chatterbot created by Fred Roberts. Freerice allows players to donate to charities by playing multiple-choice quiz games. Linerider allows users to create a track, press play, and then see a little guy navigate the track you just created. Students will create scenery to make it more interesting. Wacky Web Tales allows students to pick a story and fill in various parts of speech. Once they have filled in the various parts of speech, they click "See Your Wacky Web Tale" to get their silly story with their chosen words. Soundation and Soundtrap allow students to create their own music. Once you investigate this page, you will be able to appreciate why students absolutely enjoy exploring these links.

Linerider Examples

Transcendental™ by TechDawg created this fabulous example of how elaborate, creative and entertaining one could get with Linerider. Go to Youtube and search linerider for more fabulous examples. My students love this example.

Student Example

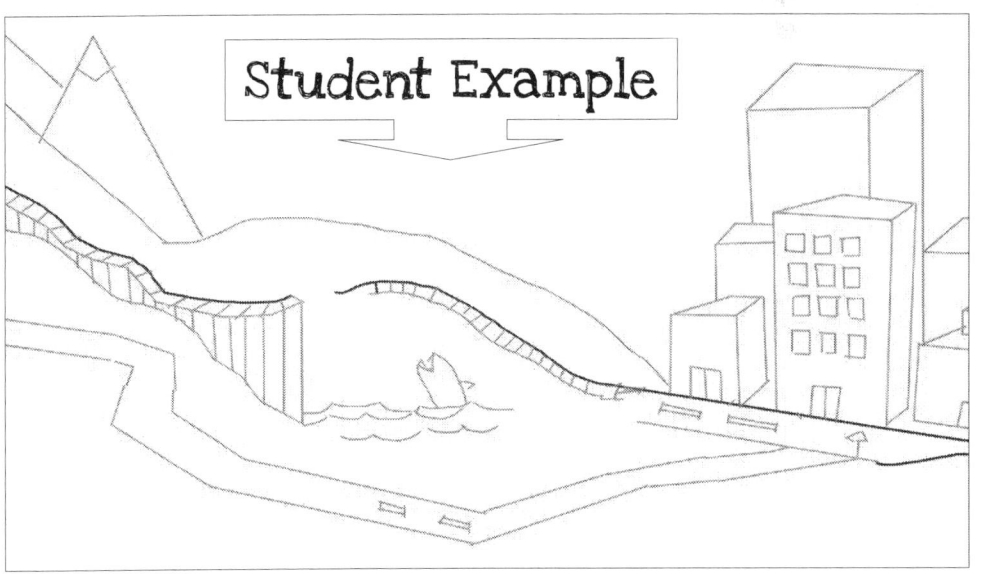

Freerice Example

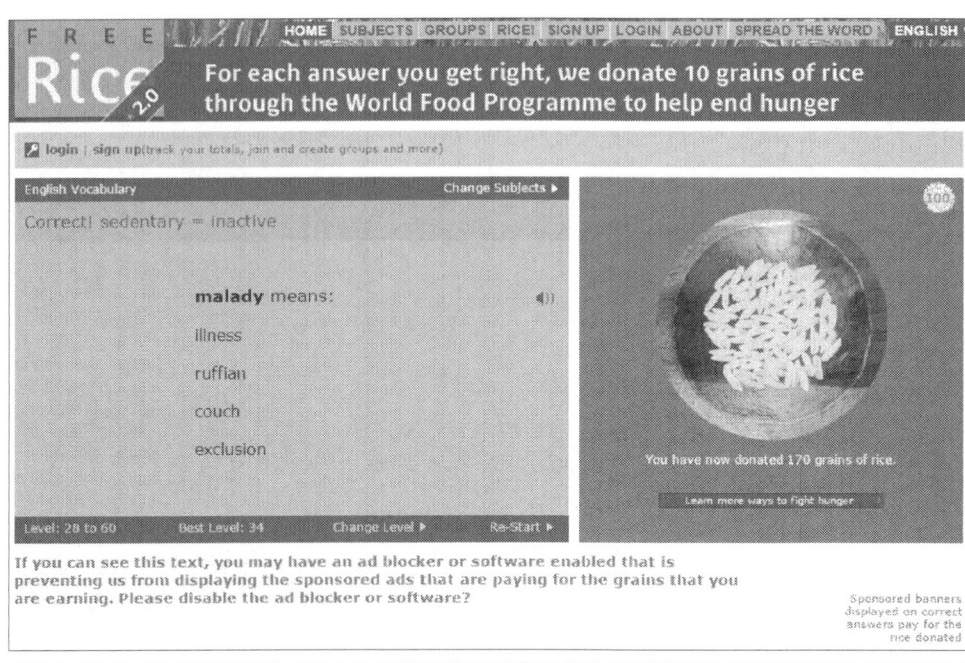

Freerice was founded in October 2007 by John Breen, a computer programmer. He said the idea came to him one day while he was preparing his older son for the SAT. He decided to create something on the computer to help his son learn vocabulary words. In March 2009, he donated the site to the UN World Food Programme. In making the donation, Mr. Breen expressed his hopes that Freerice will be able to grow over the coming years. His creation of Freerice helps feed and educate as many people as possible throughout the world. What a great concept: Learn and help those in need!

Wacky Web Tales

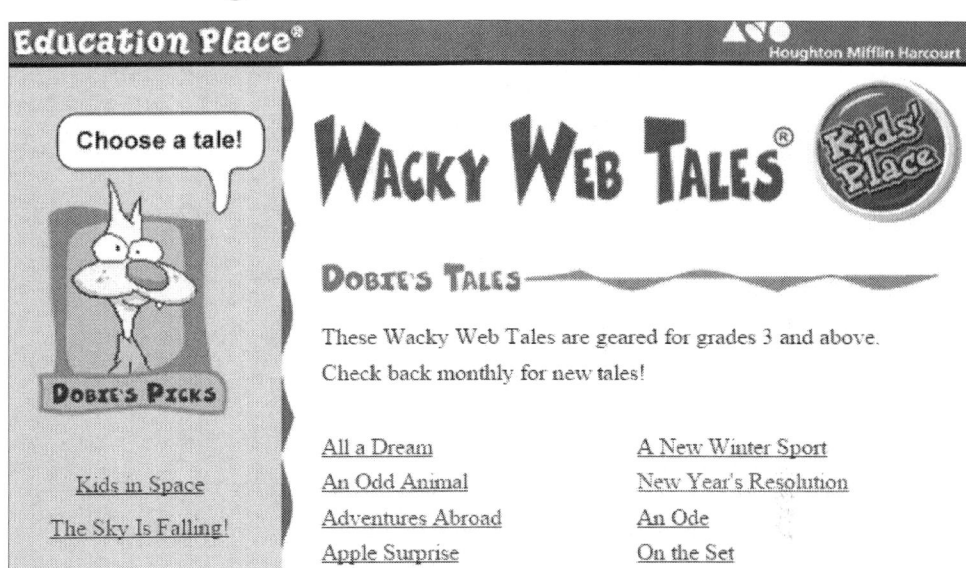

Elbot Example

Bonus Sites

If you purchase this book, you will be invited to at least three special units through your Gmail account. You will receive viewing privileges of Google Sites that are set to private. These units have many handouts, resources, videos and examples to guide students throughout production. Using these units will save you planning time, making your life easier as you provide your students fun, engaging and meaningful projects. You will have access to a PowerPoint Quotes unit, an animation unit and a funny sayings presentation unit. The animation unit is by far one of my most successful units with students. My 7th grade students enjoy this unit so much that a large percentage of them will pick my class for 8th grade. It thoroughly taps into the creativity of the students. Keep in mind that the online units will remain as current as possible. Should you find anything that needs improvement, time permitting, I will make modifications. Think of the various online units as living entities. Because you are the experts in education, your contributions are greatly appreciated. You can click on the submit link on the home page of my website to add your feedback. You can also e-mail me if you have questions. Check out the Bonus link on my site for more details.

Bonus Sites

KidsnetSoft Quotes Unit

| Home | Example | Resources | Terms | Videos |

Home

"We have forgotten how to be good guests, how to walk lightly on the earth as its other creatures do." -Barbara Ward

PowerPoint Quotes: PowerPoint is often underestimated and misunderstood. Many say it is overused. I believe you can create some wonderful products using PowerPoint. The problem is that it is used improperly just like any tool. Many presentations are done poorly. The audience is often bored with the presentation because it isn't done in a manner that maintains the attention of the audience. Design rules are ignored. This is a fun and meaningful unit that can compliment Language Arts. You can easily customize this unit for other subjects. If you are a humanities teacher, you could have your students do quotes from historical figures. I use PowerPoint with my 8th graders to do this unit. They absolutely love this project. They like looking up quotes and they enjoy finding photos to compliment the quotes. You can see the example of one of the presentations dealing with environmental quotes. I highly recommend you watch a comedian's take on PowerPoint. This lesson

"Climate change is no longer a doomsday prophecy, it's a reality." -Astrid Heiberg

Bonus Sites

Funny Presentations

| Home | Agenda | Example | Terms | Videos |

Agenda:

1. Watch the video funny movie on the Videos page or go to the Example page to see what you will be creating.

2. Create a folder and name it PowerPoint.

3. Save the funnySayings PowerPoint and the videos document into that folder to stay organized.

4. Watch the video titled getting images available for download on the Videos page. This video will help them with gathering and resizing images for this project.

5. Be sure to save all the images into the PowerPoint folder to stay organized.

6. Open the videos document and start watching and doing the videos in order. This document will help students stay organized.

7. By the time students are done watching and doing the steps in the videos, they should have a great product that is pleasant and interesting to watch.

Bonus Sites

PowerPoint Animation Unit

| Home | Example | Handouts | Terms | Videos |

Home

Welcome to the PowerPoint Animation site. This online tutorial will help you create some awesome animations using Microsoft PowerPoint. Each slide will have one thing added to make the final product look as if someone is drawing the scene on the computer. The final results are absolutely incredible. Students love this unit. They enjoy creating a variety of scenes that could end up

Handouts:

- **Creating Clipart:** This lesson is used as a pre-activity for the unit. It will help students learn how to use the tools to create drawings using the shapes in Microsoft Word or PowerPoint.

- **Kitchen**: The kitchen PowerPoint is a template. You can have students use any background they want as long as it is reasonable. The scenes should have enough detail to make the presentation interesting.

- **Kitchen Rubric**: This handout is the rubric used for this unit. You can edit it to meet the needs of your class.

- **Video Write-Ups**: This is a document to help students stay organized.

New Units

As technology continues to change and new resources become available on a constant basis, I will also get new ideas for units. I intend to add these units to the New link of my website. This is a page you might check on periodically to see if there is anything new. Every chance I get, I attend conferences on tech integration. When I attend these conferences, I tend to get fabulous ideas for different units. When this happens, I usually put together a website that tends to consist of videos, resources, examples and ideas. The New page will host those new ideas and units. This page will become its own entity. The Stem Resources & More is an example of a new resource that was added to the site while I was writing this book. This site could be used as a resource for after school clubs or for students to use if they are caught up in class and want something to explore so they can continue to learn in a fun and meaningful way. It could also be used as part of a teacher's curriculum. While writing this book, I managed to complete the Emotional Intelligence Unit. It was a great success with my 7th grade students. I can't stress enough that your feedback to improve the site is encouraged and appreciated. That link can be found on the home page of the book site at the bottom of the page. To keep it dynamic, users can <u>submit</u> changes if they see room for improvement on units.

New Units

Student Tours

| Home | Example | Resources | Tours | Videos |

Welcome to student tours. This site will provide resources for students to create tours using Tour Builder. Tour Builder allows you to show people places around the world using Google Earth. You can pick the locations right on the map. It allows you to add photos, text, and video. You can then share

Stem Resources & More

| Home | Coding | Girls | Google | iPad | Sites | Videos |

This site is set up to give students a variety of online tools to explore. It will continue to expand as more and more sites are found to help educators and students alike. This site could be used as a resource for after school clubs or for students to use if they are caught up in class and want something to explore so they can continue to learn in a fun and meaningful way. It could also be used as part of a teacher's curriculum. The Coding page has a variety of online resources for students to begin coding. The

Emotional Intelligence

| Home | Agenda | Examples | Quotes | Videos |

Home

"Emotional intelligence is the ability to identify and manage your own emotions and the emotions of others. It is generally said to include 3 skills: Emotional awareness, including the ability to identify your own emotions and those of others; The ability to harness emotions and apply them to tasks like thinking and problem solving; The ability to manage emotions, including the ability to regulate your own emotions, and the ability to cheer up or calm down another person." If you Google emotional intelligence, you will find a wealth of information and resources concluding that emotional intelligence or

Emotional Intelligence

Agenda

Directions: Complete these steps in order to have an interesting and engaging final product.

1. Are these problems? If so, how can individuals or groups of people solve these problems?
2. Define emotional intelligence.
3. Take a quiz on emotional intelligence to learn more about reading peoples' emotions.
4. Watch some examples of videos pertaining to emotional intelligence. You can download the reflection questions below (emotional intelligence videos).
5. Show an example of what students will be creating.
6. If time permits, have a class discussion on TodaysMeet about what makes a video effective?
7. After you watch and reflect on the examples, brainstorm in groups possible scenarios that could happen at school, since that is where we will be filming. You will brainstorm examples of scenarios that will demonstrate bad emotional intelligence and then good emotional intelligence. You can pick up the brainstorm document below. My students will be sharing this document in Google Docs to complete in teams.

Emotional Intelligence

Directions: Complete these steps in order to have an interesting and engaging final product.

Continued...

8. Once brainstorming has occurred, students can put together 2 or more scenarios to film on a storyboard. You can download the storyboard below.
9. Show a video demonstrating good filming so students shoot good film.
10. Once students have their film, they should complete the Animoto Setup found below.
11. With all their film and script, they can put their project together in Animoto. (Teachers can choose whatever platform they wish. The videos in steps 12-14 pertain to Animoto.)
12. Watch and do the steps of the first instructional how-to video.
13. Watch and do the steps of the second instructional how-to video to put the presentation together.
14. Watch and do the steps of the third instructional how-to video to finalize the video.

Google Apps & More

Google Apps & More is a website I put together to share with the world. I got inspired to create this site after I attended the 2014 Google Summit in Colorado. I went to some fabulous sessions and learned a great deal. I took a lot of notes and thought it would be beneficial to revisit those notes and put them on this site for others to appreciate. It helps to revisit the discussions and resources shared. By posting them on this site, it will trigger ideas for the classroom and hopefully help others make modifications for their classrooms as well. This site will continue to expand as new ideas and resources come to my attention. As I continue to attend EdTech Team Summits in Colorado or elsewhere, I will update this site. Not every session that is presented at the Summits will be represented on this site; however, I will try to highlight as many great tips as possible. There is a Google Scavenger Hunt on the Explore page that might be beneficial if you choose to explore this site in depth. This site can be a bit overwhelming because it is so packed with a variety of resources and ideas. The handout could be a way to stay a bit more focused. It could be used for teacher workshops.

Google Apps & More

Google Apps & More Site

| Home | Apps | Chrome | Drive | Ideas | Fun | Resources |

Google has some amazing and fabulous tools to assist educators in education. The tools allow students to be creative, improve literacy, collaborate and become savvier. Global Summits featuring Google for Education are continually being offered in various parts of the world, focusing on the integration of Google Apps for education. Google experts and other tech savvy educators come together to provide sessions that provide ideas, skills and expertise to promote student learning in K-12 and higher education. Google is constantly improving their apps, which will require educators dedicated to keeping up with tech integration to stay as current as possible. This site is packed with great resources. It will continue to grow as I attend Google Sessions or learn something new offered by Google. As a Computer Design teacher, I find if daunting as I try to keep up with all the changes in technology. Because I am maintaining over 40 websites, please feel free to e-mail me if you see something posted that is no longer meaningful or relevant.

Weekly Tech Tips

One time, a teacher who wasn't tech savvy came up to me and said, "My goal is to learn one new tech tip per day." I thought that was admirable. It can be tough to teach. We have to wear so many hats to be an effective teacher. I think it is imperative that teachers never stop learning. Many are afraid of tech integration. This site is designed to alleviate those fears and help them become more comfortable with the idea of incorporating technology into their curriculum. It will be populated with ideas, resources and videos to help new and seasoned teachers alike so they can become more savvy with tech integration. Technology is constantly changing and resources keep populating the Internet. I am hoping that the maintenance of this site will motivate me even more to learn as many new tips as possible to be a better teacher. You can check out the Archive page for all the tips that have been provided on this site. I will try to keep any videos under 5 minutes because time is of the essence in our field. My additional goal is to provide information that won't take more than 20 minutes to learn. Download and print the checklist to keep track of what you learn.

> "I don't use technology in my classroom because it's a buzzword or trend. I use it because connecting my kids with the world will prepare them for the future."

Weekly Tech Tips Site

KidSnetSoft Weekly Tech

Home | Archive | Check- | Feedback | Tips

Video Examples

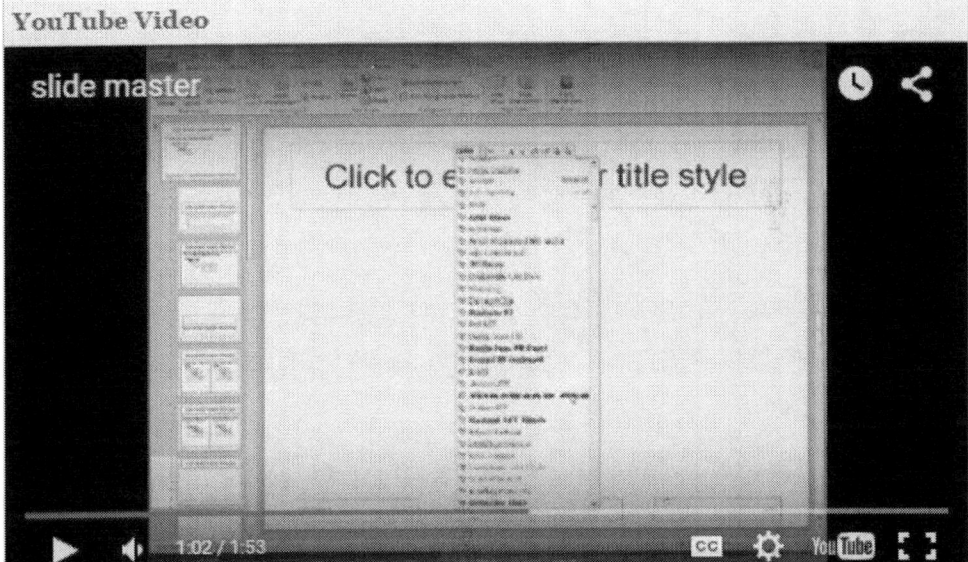

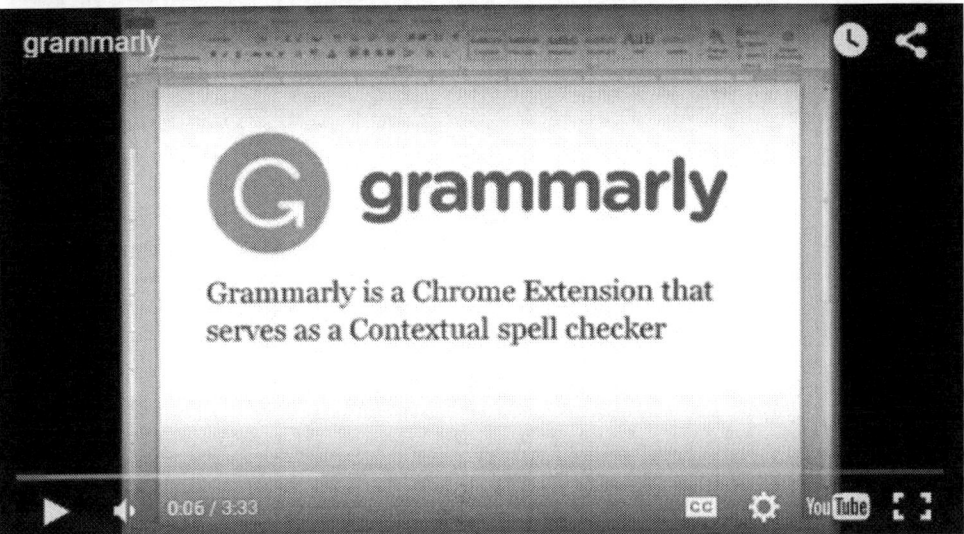

Examples of Tips

Slide Master: How to be more efficient with Microsoft PowerPoint by using the Master Slide to make modifications to design.

Google Calendar: This video shows how to create a Google Calendar. How to create events and reoccurring events.

Find Sounds: This video demonstrates how to download sounds from a site called Findsounds. It demonstrates how to download from the 3 major browsers.

Audacity: This video demonstrates how to record stories using Audacity, a free sound editing program.

Colorzilla: This video demonstrates how to use Colorzilla, a color picker that allows you to pick up colors from visually appealing websites so you can use them when creating a color scheme for your own website.

Jamendo: This video demonstrates how to download copyright friendly music for classroom projects.

Grammarly: This video demonstrates how to use Grammarly, a Chrome App, that serves as a contextual spell checker.

Examples of Tips

Any Video Converter: This free online software allows you to convert certain video formats into a variety of other different video formats. You can convert a video into audio.

Google Template: This video demonstrates how to get templates from Google to use for various classroom projects. It provides practical tips to use templates.

Translate Google: This video demonstrates how to translate a document into a different language. Though it isn't flawless, it can provide a basic foundation for communication.

Voice on Google Drawings: This video demonstrates how to record your voice using Audacity, a free sound editing program. It then illustrates how to add your recording to a Google Drawing.

Background Image: This video demonstrates how to add a background image to your Google Site. The website used for this demonstration has a variety different backgrounds that could be generated.

Tweet your Site: This video demonstrates how to add a social media interaction to your Google site.

Checklist for Tips

Teachers or students can download the checklist on the site. They can put an x under done once the video has been viewed and then provide the name of the task and a brief summary under Task to keep track of what was learned.

Done	Week	Task
	One	
	Two	
	Three	
	Four	
	Five	
	Six	
	Seven	
	Eight	
	Nine	
	Ten	
	Eleven	
	Twelve	
	Thirteen	
	Fourteen	
	Fifteen	
	Sixteen	
	Seventeen	
	Eighteen	

Notes...

Notes...

Notes...

Notes...

Notes...

Made in the USA
Middletown, DE
22 December 2017